D0899154

Also by Susan Liautaud

The Power of Ethics

The Little Book of Big Ethical Questions

Susan Liautaud

Simon & Schuster

New York   London   Toronto
Sydney   New Delhi

Simon & Schuster
1230 Avenue of the Americas
New York, NY 10020

First Simon & Schuster hardcover edition April 2022

SIMON & SCHUSTER and colophon are registered trademarks
of Simon & Schuster, Inc.

For information about special discounts for bulk purchases,
please contact Simon & Schuster Special Sales at 1-866-506-1949
or business@simonandschuster.com.

The Simon & Schuster Speakers Bureau can bring authors to
your live event. For more information or to book an event, contact
the Simon & Schuster Speakers Bureau at 1-866-248-3049
or visit our website at www.simonspeakers.com.

Interior design by Paul Dippolito

Manufactured in the United States of America

1   3   5   7   9   10   8   6   4   2

Library of Congress Cataloging-in-Publication Data
has been applied for.

ISBN 978-1-9821-3222-4
ISBN 978-1-9821-3224-8 (ebook)

To Luca, Olivia, Parker, Alexa, Cristo, and Bernard:
This is for you.

And for all of you who try hard to make ethical
choices and engage in thoughtful conversation:
my deepest admiration and hope that this book
will support you and give you the courage to
create your best stories.

Contents

CHAPTER 2: POLITICS, COMMUNITY, AND CULTURE

Contents · xi

CHAPTER 3: WORK

CHAPTER 4: TECHNOLOGY

CHAPTER 5: CONSUMER CHOICES

CHAPTER 6: HEALTH

The Little
Book of
Big Ethical
Questions

Introduction:
Ethics for Everyone

I was at a casual outdoor dinner with family and friends when someone pointed to the Impossible Burger on the menu. We all realized that despite seeing it advertised everywhere, we had no idea what was in it (soy and potatoes, with a plant-based molecule called heme for taste, created by Stanford University biochemist and Impossible Foods founder Patrick O. Brown), the true health benefits (good for a low-cholesterol or weight loss diet?), the cost (about the same as the beef burger on this menu), or environmental impact (all positive or unexpected negatives?).

How often do we find ourselves assessing the ethical stakes of day-to-day questions, from health to the environment to the economy—frequently without the information we need?

As we caught up on life and the news, and shared a taste of the Impossible Burger and some good wine, our discussion wandered from whether we were comfortable buying from a company with a track record of treating its employees poorly to the Netflix film about the college cheating scandal—*Operation Varsity Blues*—to one friend's employer now requiring Covid-19 vaccinations to return to the office . . . then back to the intensely personal . . .

questions about aging parents and a sibling's partner's secrets. The conversation was spirited and fun . . . yet thoughtful and great learning.

We confront choices every day involving ethical challenges that we don't know enough about—choices that affect our health, families and friends, work, technology, and our impact on the world. Sometimes we're alone in grappling with a question. Often these dilemmas lead to conversations with others.

The Little Book of Big Ethical Questions will guide you when you're on your own, as well as spur conversations in the company of others. Scenario by scenario the book will show you (and whomever you're talking to) how to consider your decisions even when you are confused, lack information, or feel intimidated by a complicated or cutting-edge tech issue. You don't need to be an expert: in fact, that's the point. I don't need to understand how an internal combustion engine works to know that I don't want a twelve-year-old obtaining a driver's license. I don't have to be conversant with code to worry about the potential mental health and addictive consequences of social media.

Some of the questions in the pages that follow are personal, involving family, friends, health, spirituality, emotions, or ambitions. Can we be friends with someone whose political views diverge strongly from our own? Should you take away the car keys from an elderly parent? Do you tell your best friend that their spouse is having an affair? Others are workplace dilemmas—challenges with colleagues and bosses, career choices. Should employers be able to consider a candidate's social media posts when recruiting? Should unconscious bias training be required annually? Still others relate to clarifying our opinions about the news and the world around us. Should voting be mandatory? Should we hire robots to care for the elderly? And then there are those occasions when we're called on to offer advice—considering our own views, while helping others to make the decisions they feel are best for them. The bottom line is ethics touch every aspect of our lives and our relationships. In one way or another, every decision we make matters.

My goal in this book is to *democratize ethics*: to make ethics accessible to people from all backgrounds and all walks of life; to help you experience how much power you have to make a difference in your own life and in the world around you.

The Questions

The pages that follow set out more than seventy questions to share and debate with friends, family, and colleagues—over dinner, on a Zoom call, while waiting for a train or a meeting to start, during a workout, on a walk—or to ponder on your own. All look to strengthen your *connection* with others, including those whose views differ from your own. All spur us to refine our understanding of ourselves.

Each question is paired with an exploration that includes practical points, guidance about how to prioritize what matters most, and hopeful paths forward while steering clear of blame, shame, fear, and guilt. Although organized by topic, the questions can be read in any order. The learning and insights I try to tease out in each question apply to many of the others.

Some of the questions require deeper thought. Others model "ethics on the fly"—decisions made quickly when you don't have much time, or don't need more information.

My hope is that, question by question, you will pick up themes and tips that will guide you with respect to *any* dilemma you face in your life or see on the news. You will also consider different perspectives on the issues explored that will help you shape how you view, and engage with, the world.

Some questions may seem deceptively simple at first glance. The explorations are designed to challenge the instinctive knee-jerk answer that skips over critical nuance and consequence.

I don't claim to have all the answers. In fact, often there isn't one right answer. I invite you to be my ethics sparring partner. Together we'll grapple with the issues and discover the best answers and reasoning *for you*. The questions in the book give us permission to err—while holding ourselves and others to a higher standard.

A Few Conversation Guidelines

- Don't look at these as "yes or no" questions. Look instead for the *opportunities and risks* of a decision.

- Start with *facts*. There is no such thing as alternative facts—with ethics or anything else.

- Watch for *assumptions* such as best guesses, gut instinct, relying on unverified social media posts, or confusing gossip with reliable data.

- Consider your decision from the perspective of the person most adversely affected by it. *What would it be like to be them?* Then imagine that person is you.

- Keep an *open mind*. Ethical solutions can lurk in unexpected places. And we all have *conscious and unconscious bias*.

- *Eliminate the word "perfect"* from your vocabulary. Surprisingly, striving for perfection can be a driver of unethical behavior and lead to toxic blaming, shaming, and guilt. We all err from time to time. My hand goes up first.

Sometimes we think that in grappling with ethical questions, our good character is enough. It's not: *ethics happen when character meets situations.* Whatever our character may be, we're only as ethical as our last decision.

So as you turn the pages of *The Little Book of Big Ethical Questions*, enjoy. Ponder. Share. Listen. Debate. Challenge. Trust . . . and test . . . yourself, with your friends and family, as well as in chance encounters. One conundrum at a time.

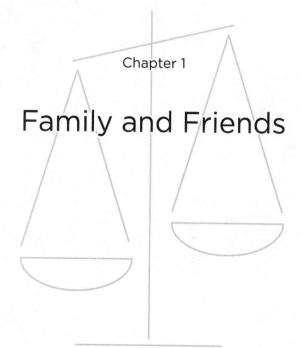

Chapter 1

Family and Friends

Could you be friends with someone whose political views differ from your own?

In the lead-up to the June 2016 Brexit vote in the United Kingdom about whether or not the United Kingdom should exit the European Union, family relationships and friendships began to show signs of stress. For some, the Brexit vote cut to the core of their—and their nation's—identity and autonomy. For others, economics, trade, the future of the younger generation, education, national security, and more were at stake. Additionally, the mix of views suffered from distorted information, fueling racism and anti-immigrant sentiments. Still, I found it difficult to believe that families were not speaking to one another, or worse, over a political matter.

Fast-forward to the highly contentious November 2020 U.S. presidential election. Many supporters of candidate Biden felt that under then President Trump we had lost our American integrity and global reputation—both the "soul of the nation" and the very foundations of democracy. Many supporters of President Trump claimed, like

Brexiteers, that American identity and "greatness" were at stake. Relationships among friends, colleagues, and family members across the country were fraying under the keenly felt strain of political polarization.

Exploration

This question probes the ethical foundations of friendship. When relationships collide with some of the most contentious issues in modern society, topics that at first might have seemed abstract rapidly become personal.

Friendship doesn't require friends to agree with each other on everything. Presumably, you didn't become friends with someone solely because of their political perspective. Friendships result in a fundamental human connection that can far outlast our political views, which can change or become outdated over time.

Moreover, expressing political views and voting constitute free speech, a pillar of democracy. Friendships (and society) are strengthened by both the exchange of ideas and engagement with people with whom we disagree— even vehemently. Information silos are one of the most powerful spreaders of unethical behavior. Doris Kearns Goodwin's award-winning biography of Abraham Lincoln, *Team of Rivals*, reminds us that our most ethical selves can emerge from intentionally engaging with those challenging our views, just as President Lincoln established a cabinet of rivals. Do we want our friendships to be judged based on how well our political views align? Or do we want to share our life experiences with humility, open-mindedness, and vulnerability? The latter option allows our friends to point out where they think we'd benefit from thinking again (even if we dig in our heels before doing so).

Recently, I must admit that this general view has challenged me more than at any other time in my life, because disregarding truth has become normal in politics. Increasingly, votes on political issues are seen as so important and defining that voting has become a choice between two sides: politics versus relationships. The distance between who we are and who our friends are, and who or what they voted for, has narrowed.

How do we reconcile our friendship with sometimes extreme politics? I believe we owe friends honesty about our own views, and the respect to not shame or condemn theirs except in extraordinary circumstances. As a practical matter, many people strike a balance with a friend whom they disagree with on a particular subject: they just don't talk about certain issues and focus instead on the many points they have in common. This is also a good approach for work, where others may feel uncomfortable engaging in discussions about politics.

There are limits, however. Because of my principles, I might part ways with a friend who goes so far as to support inciting violence or harming others. Lying about the results of a democratically held election is a close second, because if the person is willing to lie about such an important proven fact I might wonder in what other areas they ignore the truth in favor of the results they prefer.

Should you take away the car keys from an elderly parent whose driving may be unsafe?

A close friend was worried about her elderly father driving. His driving skills and attention to the road had diminished over the years. She raised her concerns with him repeatedly, but he refused to consider giving up driving. His ability to drive gave him a sense of independence that was important to him.

One day, my friend knew her father was going to the doctor for an appointment and decided to force his hand. She called the police to stop him (keenly aware that his driving would be erratic), and they arrived just as he was pulling out of the driveway. They administered a test, which he failed, so they took away his driver's license. He was unhappy, but it ultimately solved the problem.

Exploration

This question boils down to a potential conflict among key principles: safety, respect, and autonomy. Is it more important for the individual and the public to be safe, or for an individual to have the freedom and autonomy to do as they please? Other principles can be applied as well: courage, responsibility, truth, and compassionate nonjudgment. To navigate this balancing act, consider the *potential consequences* to the other stakeholders. If you don't take the keys away, are there outcomes you couldn't live with? Consider injury to your parents, and impact on anyone else on the road—not to mention *their* parents, children, and loved ones—and how you and your parents would feel if someone was badly injured.

One challenge this question spotlights is informed consent. In this case, you have all the information you need, so the "informed" part of informed consent isn't an issue. But obtaining consent—asking a parent to give up freedom, and accept the reality of age-related concerns—is challenging. For many, it's the first time an adult child may have to look after or "parent" their parents. Remind your parents of the risks and responsibilities, so they understand what is at stake. Be as specific as possible—a baby carriage being pushed across the street, a cyclist edging into the road, a jogger who crosses an intersection quickly . . . Ask them to consider how they would feel if they harmed someone else.

Even well-intentioned choices (postponing the discussion) can spread unethical behavior and breed a tolerance or normalization of potentially harmful behavior. Skewed incentives (our parent's desire to remain independent, and our desire to avoid a difficult, emotional conversation) are one force that fuels this contagion. But it is possible to create positive contagion as well, starting with having conversations with your parents or relatives about when it is the right time to stop driving . . . and hoping that others follow your good practice.

If possible, seek alternatives and blended solutions. Elderly adults can maintain autonomy by using a rideshare service, a taxi service, or public transportation. Or, if they have the resources, your parent could pay someone to drive them on a regular basis to the stores they want to patronize, a friend's house, or a religious service. A parent may also have friends who are safe drivers who can assist. Finally, you can call on the authorities as a neutral arbiter where it might help—for example, taking them for a voluntary driver's license renewal test that you're concerned they would fail.

Even easing into a difficult decision is better than doing nothing. Perhaps they will agree to no longer drive at night, or on the highway, or during rush hour. We might be under the impression that if we don't attempt to take away the car keys of an elderly parent who is no longer safe behind the wheel, we haven't made a decision. But of course, not making a decision is *also* a decision. We have decided not to intervene and leave open the possibility that they could get into a serious accident, injuring themselves—or innocent others.

Are you ethically obligated to help a neighbor?

A friend of someone I know—I'll call her Monica—lives next to an elderly woman in the Pacific Northwest. The elderly woman doesn't have much of a local support system, so one day she asked Monica for a favor. That favor has morphed into Monica driving her to doctor appointments, picking up her prescriptions, and checking in on her during the Covid-19 pandemic. Monica was torn between how much she should support her, versus how that physical support impacts the safety of her own family and children. She helped her neighbor set up a cell phone, calls her regularly, and stops in when she can.

Attempting to balance helping her neighbor with her own needs and responsibilities as a mother is a challenge. But Monica knows she would feel terrible if something happened to her neighbor because she hadn't been able to lend a hand. And she is trying to navigate whether the fact that someone lives close by matters to the ethics of our decisions—how we define "neighbor" in a Zoom-connected world.

Various books of the Hebrew and Christian bibles, from Leviticus to Galatians, from Matthew to Mark, proclaim

"Love thy neighbor as thyself." Buddhism highlights compassion and our connection to each other. The Fourteenth Dalai Lama says, "The more we care for the happiness of others, the greater our own sense of well-being becomes."

Exploration

Whatever the circumstances of your neighbor in need, in considering the question, start with an ethics triage, as if you were in an emergency room. Are the consequences of not helping a neighbor important and irreparable—such as a person falling gravely ill, or a young child being left unattended? Are you *able* to help—physically, practically, financially? For meeting many needs, living next door likely puts you in a unique position.

If you do decide to help set limits at the start: be specific about what you can and cannot do (feed the dog for three days, pick up prescriptions for the next month, or bring dinner several times, rather than "help out for a while" or "shop for food until a family member arrives from out of state"). Doing so sets expectations and establishes boundaries. If you prioritize kindness, compassion, and generosity, helping your neighbor may help reinforce the kind of person you want to be.

Nonetheless, we are not required to put ourselves at risk of harm, such as entering the home of someone with an infectious disease or stepping in to stop physical violence.

When you have fulfilled your offer to help, communicate that clearly. You are not obligated to continue. Sometimes the most effective help you can offer is to assist your neighbor in finding more sustainable alternatives—from home delivery services or maintenance providers to at-home care or other friends or family members. Or calling the authorities in the case of domestic violence.

I believe that we should try to contribute to the common good, particularly when we have the time, expertise, and resources to do so. There is an expectation that neighbors take care of one another. But no one has the resources to help everyone all of the time. And there's no right way to define what a "neighbor" is or how to contribute. The person living next door may be a relative stranger, while a friend across town (or even at the other end of a Zoom call) is more of a real neighbor than those across the street. Additionally, you may be better able to offer a particular kind of help other than the requested task. In situations like this, we can proactively propose alternative help that we *can* provide.

I avoid considering why and how someone ended up in difficulty: once someone is in need, whether because of an accident, a health problem, or an unfortunate circum-stance, the cause is less important than a forward-looking view of consequences of their situation and the provision, or not, of help. We are all susceptible of ethical mishaps. Keeping someone safe from contagious illnesses can pre-vent the spread in the wider community. Helping a neigh-bor can spur others to do the same, causing our actions to ripple outward and inspire others.

Are you ethically bound to pay for your uninsured sibling's medical care for a serious illness or accident?

David was taken aback. His older sister, whom he hadn't spoken to much in recent years apart from birthdays and holidays, had called to let him know that she had been diagnosed with breast cancer. Her oncologist wanted to schedule surgery, to be followed by extensive treatment. But what threw David even more was that his sister confided that she didn't have health insurance. A single mother with two teenage sons, she worked as a freelance publicist and didn't have much in the way of savings or retirement funds. Nonetheless, she took her kids on expensive vacations for many years. When pressed, she would tell David she was only fifty, and that she had plenty of years left.

Without health insurance, David realized that her medical bills would be more than she could handle. And she had no one else to turn to. Her marriage had ended acrimoniously, and their parents were no longer alive. When his sister talked about putting off the surgery for a few months, he felt an obligation to help out. David and his husband didn't have a lot, but he knew he could tap into his retirement account. Thinking about it made him angry, though. He and his husband had always been so frugal with their expenses, savings, and mortgage—and his sister hadn't been as responsible.

Exploration

The key issues here are your relationship with the individual (how close you are—or not), kinship (however you define family, not limited to biological relationships), how deserving you feel someone is of help, and your own financial situation.

Health care in the U.S. is a complicated mix of private employer-sponsored plans and government programs. According to the U.S. Census Bureau, in 2019 55.4 percent of Americans get their health care coverage through their jobs. Senior citizens who are sixty-five and over are covered through the federal Medicare program while those with low incomes receive help from federal Medicaid programs. Still others buy subsidized health care through the Affordable Care Act (Obamacare) marketplaces. But it's a patchwork system, and ultimately not everyone has, or can afford, health care—the Census Bureau reports that 26.1 million people did not have health insurance in 2019. In other developed countries such as the United Kingdom, obtaining lifesaving medical care is not left up to the individual. As of 1948, virtually every citizen in the U.K. is covered by the National Health

Service, which offers comprehensive health care through the government.

We are under no obligation to underwrite another's health care, whether a family member or not. We are not ethically responsible to make up for an inadequate health care system, or to do harm to ourselves in the name of helping others. Only you can assess your capacity and your desire to help. Every situation is unique, and this decision also requires considering how our resources and needs may change over time.

If you're unsure of your answer, there are a few other questions that can help. Is the illness so serious or severe that expensive treatment is the only option? Does it matter to you if your sibling could have obtained medical insurance but did not? Or led an unhealthy lifestyle? Or could have saved money but instead splurged on luxuries? If you do decide to help financially, clarify limits on your generosity up front—the amount and whether this is an outright gift or a loan.

If you'd like to help, but are financially unable, there are other avenues to explore. Perhaps your sibling can secure a loan or other family members can help share the financial burden. You may be able to help research other sources of aid, provide assistance navigating the health care system, or offer support in other ways, like driving them to appointments or delivering groceries. But it's a personal choice, and only you can know what is right for you.

Should you read your child's or teenager's diary or journal?

Years ago, I saw a story in the news about a well-meaning mother who regularly read her fifteen-year-old's diary. She thought it would offer insight into why their conversations were so fraught with anger. Similarly, a friend of mine secretly reads her son's diary because she is concerned about his "extremely erratic behavior." She shares the contents with her therapist, but no one else. Her justification is that she has tried unsuccessfully to discuss her concerns with him. She has never read the diaries of her other children. Nonetheless, she worries that she is modeling disrespect and betrayal—and if she is discovered, won't be forgiven. But then she pushes the thought away, sighing, "Teenagers don't have perspective."

Anne Frank's diary, published as *The Diary of a Young Girl*, is one of my favorite books of all time. It chronicles a young Jewish girl and her family, hiding in the attic of another Dutch family in Amsterdam for several years, trying to escape the Holocaust. Published posthumously—Anne Frank died in the Bergen-Belsen concentration camp in

1945—her diary is said to be the most widely read nonfiction book in the world other than the Bible. It reveals the fears, hopes, infatuations, and inner life of a young girl caught up in the horror of Nazi Europe. And it reminds us that diaries act not only as literary records of our thoughts, but also as tools for navigating life.

Exploration

I'm not a mental health professional or parenting guru (I'm a highly imperfect mother of five young adults), and every situation is unique. But this question often triggers guilt and defensiveness, and in my view there's little productive place in ethics for either. In the midst of day-to-day parenting, we often lose perspective. Ethics can help us reason through the emotion and shift 20/20 hindsight to problem-solving foresight.

A child's diary is a private sanctuary, whether online or on paper, whether it is conveyed in words, drawings, or photographs. A diary serves as a healthy outlet to express one's deepest emotions, dreams, and ideals. Let's be clear. Reading a child's diary without their knowledge or permission is dishonest, disrespectful, and a violation of privacy. It undermines trust, as does any form of dishonesty. It's possible that if your actions are discovered you could push your child or teenager to withhold even more, which could have lasting effects on your relationship with them.

But ethical questions are rarely "yes or no," "black or

white" dilemmas. I like to ask the question: *When—and under what circumstances—should we act?* When might you compromise honesty due to concern for your child's well-being? How do other principles like privacy, safety, respect, and truth factor into your decision? What is the result you're trying to reach? Imagine looking back on your decision a month, a year, five years down the line, and ask yourself: Will my justifications still make sense once more time has passed? To me, the most compelling reasons to read a child's diary without permission are health and safety—of the child and others.

One way to look at this is to consider other instances where privacy and confidentiality are involved. At one extreme, medical professionals are permitted to violate doctor-patient confidentiality if they believe someone's life is at stake. Contracts may not be airtight: society is less and less tolerant of enforcing nondisclosure agreements signed by victims of sexual misconduct, because they allow perpetrators to continue with impunity. On the other hand, a parent's mere curiosity is not justification to compromise honesty or respect; as my research assistant says, there's a "difference between concerned and nosy." Intrusive or controlling parenting is not an excuse for dishonesty.

Consider other alternatives first—speaking to your child about your concerns, or perhaps getting professional advice to determine whether the red flags you are seeing are as serious as you think. Ask yourself if there are other ways you might discern whether your child's safety is at risk. If you do decide it is necessary to read their diary, only share the contents with confidentiality-bound professionals who can help guide you.

Children often don't have perspective on how serious their situation is—or the type of help that might be available.

Would you give someone who has wronged you several times another chance?

Perhaps your mother continually breaks confidences with you by telling other family members about your problems. Or your supervisor consistently takes credit for work you have done. Or your teenage daughter lies about things she did, or didn't do, like claiming she was at the library while she was really at a party drinking.

The closer the individuals are to us (a spouse, child, relative, or close friend as opposed to an occasional friend or professional colleague), the more we have to lose emotionally, socially, and sometimes materially when there's a breach of trust. We may feel ethically responsible for attempting to maintain the relationship, or continuing to support the other person—but what's our obligation?

Exploration

We've all been there: someone lied to us, cheated on us, betrayed a confidence, or has been consistently irresponsible or unreliable. We may have the old proverb "fool me once, shame on you; fool me twice, shame on me" lingering in the back of our minds. How would we approach repairing the relationship—and should we?

In order to recover from ethics transgressions—reconcile a past wrong inflicted on you in this case—the other person needs to tell you the full truth, take responsibility for their actions, and assure you that the behavior will not be repeated. Establishing their trustworthiness is the foundation for future connection. Start by asking whether you have the information you need to consider the ethics of the decision. You need to know what the *other person* knew. Did they know that their behavior was ethically wrong? Should they have? If you have talked with them after previous missteps, they had all the information they needed to make an ethical choice—and they chose not to. What might have been a mistake the first time becomes intentional when it is repeated—especially the third or fourth time. Is there reason to believe their behavior will change in the future?

Then consider the danger of impunity. If you continue to tolerate unwanted behavior, you remove incentives to improve, and you may become part of the problem as an enabler.

Perhaps you decide to continue to engage with them, but only in limited ways—for example, in a work environment (where you may not have much of a choice), you might continue to be respectful and act professionally, but no longer treat them as a trusted colleague or friend.

There are times when gut-wrenching decisions about our most important relationships are at stake—leaving a cheating spouse when you have children and no place to go. Or choosing to let an adult child stand on their own after repeated incidents of dishonesty or misconduct.

What if someone is struggling with health issues—can we make the argument that "they can't help it"? For example, people suffering from addiction are battling a tragically difficult disease. We might call on our compassion more than we would in the case of hurtful behavior from someone who is well. The same goes for someone struggling with mental health issues. But that doesn't mean that we have to live with these individuals or continue to support them in everything. In cases like these, we can set boundaries on the relationship.

Conversely, physical or verbal abuse, dangerous behavior involving weapons, dealing or using illegal drugs, and drunk driving—these are all deal breakers, in my view. In such cases, other considerations such as safety override everything else.

Finally, there is often confusion between forgiveness and ethical recovery. Many wise people say that forgiveness is for the forgiver. It's about moving on; it's not about changing the other person's behavior. However, ethics recovery requires the other person to change: telling the truth, taking responsibility, and committing to different future behavior. Second (or third) chances cannot take place without their agreeing to all three.

Are you obligated to give all your children equal shares of your estate?

conic French rock star Johnny Hallyday (known as the French Elvis) passed away in 2017, having left his two biological adult children out of his will—in violation of French law. After a sordid media battle between the children and Hallyday's wife at the time of his death, the adult children prevailed in court and were awarded part of his estate.

Most families do not have their succession play out in court or the media, but we do face questions of how to distribute our worldly belongings. How do ethics matter when deciding what children with different sized families— or no children at all—should receive? What if one child is wealthy, while another is struggling to pay the rent? What if one has a bigger family or costly medical needs? Should personal preference be a factor?

Exploration

The question is highly personal, cultural, and, in some cases, even religious. I clarify a few ethics threads, but in most cases, there is no right or wrong answer here. We don't owe anyone our possessions (or our attention, time, letters of recommendation, loans, friendship, love, organs)—in life or in death.

There is an important distinction between equal (the same share to each) and equitable (fair and impartial). In some cases, equal may not seem fair and fair may not seem impartial. You will need to decide what principles are important to you, and how you can apply them.

Let's consider the question of inheritance on a spectrum.

At one extreme, in France, the Napoleonic Code, introduced in 1804, limits one's freedom on bequeathing assets, except for property held abroad: everything from apartments to bank accounts to favorite handbags is divided up among children in accordance with legally mandated percentages tied to the number of children, as the court decided in the case of Johnny Hallyday.

At the other extreme, there are ethical wills, which harken back to centuries-old Jewish and Muslim tradition, but today are used by people of all faiths. They pass on ethical principles and priorities from one generation to the next. You might leave your commitment to humility and compassion to child A, your love of people and volunteering to child B. They are fascinating add-ons to formal wills, although they don't determine distribution of material possessions.

Between these extremes, most of us decide for ourselves how to divide our material possessions.

You can't predict how your children and others will respond, but you can start with two pillars: responsibility and transparency. Responsibility: Do you have children that you are still legally responsible for (or feel responsible for)—perhaps one is battling an illness or has special needs, or is caring for children with special needs? Transparency: consider telling your adult children of your estate plans so you can manage their expectations, and that any questions or conflicts can surface while you are still alive.

You may also consider what has been given already. In the case of children who assumed the role of caregiver to you, potentially forgoing income, perhaps now is the time to pay them back in kind. Additionally, it may be helpful to consider what you've given your various children during their lifetimes: education, loans, weddings.

Ethics do not offer a one-size-fits-all answer, nor do they guarantee family harmony. Conversations around money and family are often fraught with emotion. But starting with responsibility and transparency helps distill the ethics stakes in your situation and can offer a foundation for your conversations. And of course we have the right to change our decision over time.

Would you use direct-to-consumer genetic testing kits?

You hear a friend has purchased a 23andMe kit. You're intrigued and would like to find out more about your family's ancestry. You don't fully understand what you will learn from the kit, but you're also curious about your health and genetic history.

Many of us have seen the direct-to-consumer (DTC) genetic testing kits advertised in media ranging from Oprah's Favorite Things to *People* magazine. And it's easy to do: order the kit, spit into a vial, and send it to the company. Then wait to discover the results. Teenagers think of it as a great gift idea, and parents are using it with their children. Technically, AncestryDNA and 23andMe require users to be eighteen years of age, but parents can do the tests "on behalf of . . . those for whom [they] have legal authority." According to *MIT Technology Review*, the total number of people in the databases of 23andMe, AncestryDNA, and several smaller companies grew to more than 26 million people by the beginning of 2019.

After checking, you see that among the range of

information you might uncover using 23andMe are insights about your health (an increased risk of certain diseases), ancestry (origins and relationship to "groups of people . . . across the globe"), and family (paternity, such as your biological father not being who you thought he was). These kits can provide important opportunities if used thoughtfully.

Exploration

The central question is whether there are irreparable consequences or *potential* consequences to consumers learning the information they may obtain from DTC genetic testing kits. Autonomy (the right to know and the right *not to know*), privacy, health, and safety are all at stake here. Perhaps the most critical: *you cannot un-know information once you have learned it.*

Ordinarily, information concerning your health and the health of your family would be kept confidential. But here, as 23andMe warns on its website, "genetic information that you share with [others] may be used against your interests," and their privacy policies can change at any point. If insurance companies access this data, or require you to provide it, they could decide not to cover you or raise the cost of insurance.

Then there's the unpredictability of how you will react—for example, if you discover you have the gene for a serious disease such as cancer. In the case of teenagers or children, processing the implications of health information could bring confusion and distress. In my view, children under eighteen should not be made responsible for decisions about sharing or not sharing genetic information that could affect others.

DTC kits can dismantle one of the long-standing pillars of ethics—informed consent. As adults we consent for ourselves. With teenagers, parents consent for them. This deprives them of the right to decide for themselves when they are older. They may learn something at a young age that, when they're an adult, they wouldn't have chosen to know. Or vice versa. Worse, in some situations, using DTC kits could lead to exposing others who have no opportunity to consent (a spouse who learns they are not the child's parent, siblings learning of a genetic disease, even family members of criminals caught using DTC kit results uploaded on various sites).

In medically prescribed genetic testing, the patient would have a professional walk them through the decision— the reasons for the test, the scope of information required, and the risks and benefits of possible outcomes. Likely, the tests would be limited to those necessary to the medical matter at hand. DTC kit technology eliminates the professional filter between you and potentially life-altering knowledge.

Our ethical responsibility is even greater when there is no driving imperative to do DTC genetic testing and there are alternatives. Doctors can recommend and supervise targeted (and possibly more accurate) tests for specific health concerns. The American Society of Human Genetics encourages parents to defer predictive testing for children for adult-onset diseases until adulthood, or "the child is an older adolescent who can participate in decision-making in a relatively mature manner."

If you're planning to send in your DNA, or the DNA of your child, read the fine print and detailed disclosure they provide and then pause to reflect on its implications. And remember, whatever a company's terms of service, they can change. Better yet, seek a professional opinion *before* you use the kit rather than waiting until after you have obtained the results.

Would you tell your friend information about their fiancé you think they should know before getting married?

Your best friend is engaged to be married. You want to be thrilled, but although you've met your friend's fiancé a number of times, something about them makes you feel uneasy, as if they are hiding something or acting in a way that doesn't seem entirely honest. But you keep it to yourself because, after all, it's just a feeling.

But then you stumble upon a more specific concern—a transgression, a lie—that confirms your worst fears. And you're pretty sure your friend knows nothing about it. Perhaps you discovered that the person cheated on your friend. Or lied about their financial situation. You're not sure if you owe it to your friend to tell them. The thought of bringing this new information to your friend, and possibly ruining their happiness, is terrifying. But what if you don't tell your friend, and he or she discovers it later once they are married?

Exploration

First, separate the ethics question from your opinion about your friend's partner. You may need to act if your friend (or someone else) is at risk of harm, or if you know of behavior on the part of their fiancé that violates their core values such as abuse, a hidden addiction, history of lies, or mistreatment of others. A general dislike or feeling that your friend's intended is "just not good enough" is not an ethics matter.

At the same time, you can use ethics to guide what you view as your responsibility as a friend. In relationships, for me these considerations may include honesty, compassion, transparency, and loyalty.

Ask yourself, *Why do I feel compelled to tell them?* Is it out of concern for their well-being? Is it so that your friend has all the information needed to make the right decision for them? The more precise you can be about the issue, and the clearer you are about your goals, the easier it will be to share your concerns, and for your friend to be able to hear them. And the more you'll stay in your ethics lane.

Check first that your information is accurate. You can approach the fiancé, asking them to clarify the situation and giving them the opportunity to tell your friend first. If that doesn't seem possible, tell your friend how you came across this information (that's part of transparency). Any time we are a bystander, there's a risk that we may not know the full story and could cause unintended harm.

Focus only on the concern—not condemning the other

person. Avoid gossip. Share information privately with your friend to give them space to react without others present. Again, you're not trying to suggest the right decision for your friend—only to give them the information they need to make sure they make the right decision for themselves, and for you to fulfill your obligations as a friend.

Consider also whether you are willing to live with the consequences of telling your friend (or not). Of course, your friend could be extremely upset, whatever you decide. Some might not want to risk a friendship by telling their friend upsetting news. But what if your friend finds out, years later, that you knew and didn't tell them? They may feel betrayed by your lack of transparency.

Most importantly, consider your friend's point of view: What would your friend want to know, based on the history of your friendship? When your friend responds, listen to what they tell you—not what you want or expect to hear. Remember, this is not about you. The fact that life, and our decisions, don't have perfect outcomes doesn't mean we aren't doing our best ethically.

What are the differences between a white lie and a serious ethical transgression?

Recently, during the Q&A after a talk I gave, a member of the audience who was in the process of selling her house asked whether she was ethically obligated to tell her real estate agent and the buyer about any negative experiences she had had with the house. Another audience member asked me whether it was okay to embellish her accomplishments on a dating website. A third audience member asked about lying to the police about why she had been speeding.

Exploration

These kinds of questions essentially ask when and under what circumstances distorting the truth is acceptable—if ever.

To me, truth is a nonnegotiable foundation for ethical decision making. Without truth, we violate ethical commitments like honesty, integrity, empathy, and transparency. We lack the accurate information we need to consider who will be affected by our decisions and how. There is no such thing as alternative facts when it comes to ethics.

There is a pattern in the examples above: we're consciously acting out of self-interest to get someone to *make a choice that we don't think they would make if they knew the truth.* We want someone to purchase our house, go out on a date with us, or give us a pass on a speeding ticket. In other words, getting someone else to agree to what we want based on *distorted truth.* We can contrast that with the white lies we sometimes tell to avoid hurting others' feelings—"You haven't aged a day!" or "I love that dress." In these cases the other person is not using our information to make a choice. Put differently, we are expressing an opinion, not stating (or misstating) a fact.

All of these stories spotlight the danger of contagion of falsity, whether by commission or omission. The danger is that compromised truth can become a habit. It becomes normalized and, over time, we up the ante, confusing self-interest with a legitimate rationale.

You don't owe the purchaser of your house disclosure of every detail. But regardless of the law, you do owe them honesty about issues significant enough to affect their decision to purchase the house at the price you set. Most real estate sales are contingent upon the house passing an inspection by a professional and your representations of the house. If the buyer discovered a major flaw post-closing, you could be held liable under the contract. You might also ask yourself, aside from what is legal, is this something *I* would want to know if I were in the buyer's position?

We all know people frequently distort the truth on dating apps. Chipping a few years off your age or lying about your interests are intended to get a foot in the door. These lies are intentional, to influence the other person's choice. The people who do it know they are not being truthful and those lies often come out later. Acknowledging and apologizing for a falsehood is a lot harder than telling the truth the first time, because it not only reveals the lie, it also shows that you are someone who isn't completely trustworthy. A person may think: *What else might this person lie about?*

It goes without saying that lying to a police officer or other official is unwise. Moreover, it also says that you are prepared to violate two of our culture's most fundamental principles: truth and safety. Driving above the speed limit is a mistake that many of us make—an ethics failure (whether or not intentional) because it puts us and others at risk. But lies are an *intentional* failure of ethics.

Would you violate your teenager's confidence if not doing so might lead to harm?

Perhaps your teenager confided in you about a friend who has been using and selling drugs—swearing you to absolute secrecy. Or you found some pills in your teenager's possession that had been given by a friend to increase concentration for upcoming exams.

You know that if you break a promise, your teenager's trust could be undermined, as well as their willingness to share future information. It can also set in motion other dangerous behaviors (including lying or hiding the truth). On the other hand, if you don't speak up, harmful behavior could continue unchecked. Innocent people could be hurt.

Exploration

Dilemmas that pit confidentiality against other ethics guideposts, such as safety and responsibility, happen all too often.

Explain to your child in clear terms that you feel you must break confidentiality *in this particular case* and *why*. By asking permission, you transform your request from a broken promise into a situation-specific exemption from your promise. In contrast, if you lie about or hide your intentions, your actions are a violation of the confidentiality you promised.

Consider whether there are more options (i.e., beyond tell or don't tell). For example, urge your child to convince their friend to come clean or stop the behavior. (This works better for adults, as it may burden your child with a lot of responsibility.) Or you can obtain your child's agreement to share some, but not all, of the information. Explain exactly what you would share with surgical precision: the least amount of information to the fewest number of people, with a very specific goal in mind.

If your child refuses to give permission, you might talk to the parents of the other child, keeping the conversation general, or consult a doctor or counselor for further advice. ("Many students are trying this new drug X, and nobody knows where it's coming from.") In the end, you may feel you have to violate your child's confidentiality, but you will have been honest and transparent.

Before acting, assess the credibility of the information you have: the source, the level of detail, and the quality (an eyewitness account versus gossip). Be sure it's a serious matter, like one involving illegal drugs, driving under the influence, or cheating that could result in expulsion. Weigh the immediate and longer-term consequences, including others who may potentially be affected by the situation: a friend, an innocent victim of drugs or a car accident, and the other person's family. If you know of potential harm and say nothing, you bear some responsibility if it transpires. Do whatever you can to eliminate any risk of harm to your child, such as forbidding your child to get in a car with a friend who drinks and drives. Finally, encourage them to consult with medical, legal, and mental health providers and religious advisors whose confidentiality obligations are both legally binding and based on professional ethics.

If you decide to tell the child's family, remember that they may not welcome the information. You cannot control the other person's response—only your own. Put yourself in their shoes: How would you feel if someone told *you* this? On the other hand, how would you feel looking back on your decision after the worst had already happened? Or how would you feel if someone else knew of a serious issue with your child and didn't tell you?

We are being asked here to consider more than just whether it is our story to tell. We are being asked whether it is a story we can afford *not* to tell.

Would you call the police on a friend you fear might drive under the influence of alcohol?

have a dear friend whose spouse regularly drinks too much in social settings—at parties, at restaurants on some occasions, at sporting events. Yet despite the fact he's had too much to drink to drive safely, he will get behind the wheel of his car to drive home, claiming he is only traveling "locally." Which is true, but "locally" refers to a big city with complex traffic patterns and varied speed limits—and ignores the fact that he shouldn't be behind the wheel of a car anywhere in his condition. If he is with his wife, she will drive. But sometimes he is on his own.

Here are a few chilling statistics for perspective: it's illegal to drive with a blood alcohol level of .08 g/dL or higher in every state in the U.S. (except Utah, where the limit is .05 g/dL). That is roughly equal to three drinks for most people, depending on their weight and the amount of time that has transpired. In 2019, according to the

National Highway Traffic Safety Administration, 10,142 people in the U.S. died in a drunk-driving accident—one person every fifty-two minutes. In 2019, 28 percent of all fatal car accidents in the U.S. involved a driver who had been drinking.

Exploration

This question appears to pit ethical principles against each other—safety of the driver and innocent people versus the loyalty and confidentiality of our friendship. Let's start with what I call 20/20 foresight. Catapult yourself into the future: looking back on your decision in a month, a year, five years, how would you feel if someone was injured because you didn't try to stop your friend? Would you feel differently if nothing happened? Assuming our sources are reliable, or we've witnessed our friend's behavior for ourselves, we have all the information we need to make an ethical decision. If you lose a loved one to a drunk driver, you don't care whether it was the driver's first offense or a habitual pattern of abuse.

First, I would do everything that I could to change the situation directly, from telling my friend unequivocally not to drive, to reaching out to a partner to come and pick them up, to persuading my friend to wait for a few hours at least until they are sober enough to drive.

If your friend is about to get behind the wheel, and others fail to act, you may need to involve the authorities. Alerting the police about the drunk driving of a friend could result in your friend being arrested. While this could cost you the friendship, the consequences of not doing so could be far worse. And loyalty in my view does require trying to prevent a friend from making a life-altering mistake.

The more difficult situation involves a chronic drinker. You're not always there to intervene. Speak to your friend—maybe they're not aware of how much they are drinking. Failing that, speak to family members or a partner. The point here is to urge them to seek a lasting solution to protect their own safety and the safety of others—not to preach, criticize, or shame. Police generally do not engage in these situations because there is not an imminent criminal act.

People struggling with addiction are battling a disease. Compassion and humility are in order, but we don't owe them blind loyalty, such that we enable them to do harm.

We should ask how we might allow for earlier, confidential, safety-focused ways to report fears of someone *about* to drive under the influence—perhaps resulting in a warning with no permanent consequences unless there are multiple offenses. I don't have a perfect solution. But I have seen repeatedly how official but non-threatening options for reporting potential wrongdoing can increase willingness to seek help and offer a life- or career-saving wake-up call.

In the end we can't control what our friends do. And

let's circle back to the idea that safety and loyalty might conflict here: if we do feel compelled to call the police, hopefully our friend will realize that our principles in fact align. Their safety and their best long-term interests are both expressions of our loyalty.

Would you pay, or allow teachers to pay, your children to study or read books?

You discover that the parents of one of your ten-year-old's classmates pay him $20 for every A he earns. Another family incentivizes their child by giving money for every completed homework assignment. A third uses the stick rather than the proverbial carrot—they won't let their child play sports or have play dates unless she achieves certain grades. The high school English teacher of your older child, to bring up the lower-performing end of the class, is rewarding students by giving them $5 for every grade improvement. (You have no idea whether the lower-performing students come from more difficult or less privileged home environments. Nor do you know if the teacher receives a bonus or other benefits for class grades.) These are a mix of real situations I saw as a parent.

Exploration

Are the efforts described above legitimate strategies to incentivize students or simple bribery? Cheating? Mundane parenting tactics like threatening to take the phone away if they use inappropriate language, or offering TV time in exchange for extra household chores? Is something being sold that shouldn't be sold? If so, what?

The *Oxford Advanced Learner's Dictionary* defines cheating as "act[ing] in a dishonest way in order to gain an advantage." Cheating violates principles like honesty, fairness, and equity, and is unacceptable. But most parents I have met over the years are not trying to obtain an unfair advantage—they simply want to incentivize learning. Education is not an even playing field, with or without parental inducements.

Next, is something for sale that shouldn't be sold, like friendship, kidneys, or sex, as Harvard University professor and political philosopher Michael Sandel intriguingly asks in a lecture he gave at the Oxford Union. If you think education is for sale here, bear in mind that we sell education all the time—through university fees, private nursery schools, property taxes for public schools, or paying for ballet lessons and math camps. Is there much difference between paying your child $5 per book read and hiring private tutors and coaches?

In my view, we're not buying or selling education, but rather motivation and effort. The child doesn't lose the underlying good—education. On the contrary, they gain it. One clear guideline in my view: We *shouldn't* pay for ethical conduct like telling the truth, showing respect, and being honest and compassionate. *Ethics are not for sale*. Doing well in school, however, is not an ethical principle. Many morally upstanding people do not excel in the classroom, the way I fail miserably at many sports. And they might do better—and learn better—with incentives. Still, Sandel makes a critical point that markets, and the economics underpinning choice, should not function independently of morality.

One of the students in Sandel's audience argued that if the payment incentivizes the child to read more, it is a small price to pay to jump-start a lifetime of learning. Others argue that children will miss the joy of discovering reading for themselves. Perhaps most importantly, reading is a fundamental life skill regardless of parental ambitions or enjoyment—and an indicator of the egregious inequality in our society. Considering the benefits of reading young, the harm of parents using financial transactions to encourage creating those benefits may seem small.

Teachers have to balance motivation, discipline, incentives, and a love for learning. There is no way to be truly fair about choosing which students to pay as teachers can never know the full story of what's going on at home. Because of that, I don't support teachers giving students money for anything. That said, I very much admire teachers and sympathize with the challenge of being attentive to their students' diverse learning needs.

Would you tell—or want to be told—about an affair?

Some years ago I was at a casual dinner with a group of friends, and the question arose as to what we would do if we found out that a close friend's spouse was having an affair. Would we tell our friend? A few in the group said they would. They also would want to know if their own spouse was having an affair and would end the marriage immediately. One friend whose husband traveled constantly on business answered, "I wouldn't want to know. As long as he comes home on Friday night, I want my life, my children's lives, and our home life protected. If someone tells me, I'd have to respond—and maybe be judged if I don't throw him out or act the way others think I should." She felt that even if others knew, as long as she didn't know, she wasn't responsible for having to face painful life decisions. Still others, while not condoning affairs, wrestled with whether they would tell and wondered if they would want to be told. One wanted to be told, but didn't care if her spouse was having an affair.

Exploration

To start, let's clarify whose ethics we are talking about. Our own principles don't apply to other people's relationships. People are free to manage their relationships with their own ethics. Individuals decide their principles and make practical compromises all the time—whether putting up with an affair, sacrificing emotional intimacy, or doing a disproportionate share of the housework.

So let's stay focused on our own ethics. How do *our* principles—and how they play out in our friendship—relate to whether or not we tell? My answer rests on one mantra-like question: *Is it your story to tell?* And a corollary: Your friend *cannot un-know* information once you tell them.

The first step is to make sure we have the information we need to make an ethical choice. Are you sure that what you think is true is true? Unless one of the parties having the affair told you (ideally, both of them told you), you may not know as much as you think. Even if you do have reliable firsthand information, no one can know what is going on in someone else's marriage. Maybe your friend already knows and is trying to work it out quietly, or is suffering with the knowledge but is not ready to share.

More important, it's not your information, your truth, or your story to tell. It's theirs. You won't be the one living with the consequences. So I try my best to be careful about making choices that affect the people who will be living with them. If your friendship is based on honesty, transparency, and loyalty, you may feel that you need to share this.

Fair enough—again assuming you have thought through the caveats. Perhaps try testing the water a bit; ask your friend whether everything is okay at home.

I almost always ask how we would feel in the shoes of the person most adversely affected by our decision—a query that calls up our empathy, compassion, and humility. Whether or not you would want to know is irrelevant; what matters is what you believe your friend would want. Even if you think you know or heard your friend's views in a theoretical dinner discussion, when we are living through an ethical conundrum ourselves, we may not be so sure. For example, I wouldn't assume that my friend's dinner commentary a while ago would reflect their wishes if their spouse was cheating today.

In most cases, there is no driving imperative to reveal information here. You are not a bystander to someone who is in danger, as would be the case, for example, if you were witnessing imminent danger like physical abuse. Asking whether it's your story to tell applies to so many areas of life. Seemingly harmless information can become significantly more perilous when shared. If you share it, you assume some responsibility for the consequences of that sharing.

Would you return the extra change?

I had the privilege of interviewing Rob Chesnut, former chief ethics officer of Airbnb. I started by asking him where he got his true north . . . his own set of ethical principles that have guided him personally and throughout his successful legal and ethics career. Without hesitation, he praised his mother. He recalled an experience as a young child. He and his mother were leaving the supermarket when his mother discovered the cashier had mistakenly given her some extra change. She turned around, with her son in tow, and went back inside to return the money. Today, this act may seem quaint, but it stuck with me as an example of how one small act can set an example for a lifetime of ethical behavior.

As I was preparing for the interview, I read a graduation speech given by retired Navy four-star Admiral William H. McRaven, then the chancellor of the University of Texas. McRaven had been the commander of the U.S. Special Operations Command who oversaw the Navy SEALs' successful raid that killed Osama bin Laden. His commencement speech became the anchoring story in a subsequent bestselling book, *Make Your Bed*. Admiral McRaven advised that making your bed "will encourage you to do another task and another and another. By the end of the day, that one task completed will have turned into many tasks completed. Making your bed will also reinforce the fact that little things in life matter. If you can't do the little things right, you'll never be able to do the big things right."

"If you want to change the world," McRaven advised, "start off by making your bed. . . ."

Exploration

This question asks us to consider when, whether, and why little things matter. It asks us to press pause and think about our day-to-day decisions, what I consider our "ethics housekeeping." It probes how we draw lines: What's worth worrying about?

Rob Chesnut's childhood story describes one of those rare "yes or no" moments. We shouldn't leave with money that doesn't belong to us. It doesn't depend on the situation. But we often rationalize our actions away—"It's too small an amount to be worth the effort to go back inside to return it" or "It doesn't matter to the store or even the cashier." But like many seemingly mundane ethical moments, the lessons are far-reaching.

Small transgressions can be cumulative. They become habits. And the thinking can spread to other areas. Just as shoddy bed making can lead to leaving more important things undone, leaving with money that isn't yours can lead to seemingly minor ethical missteps, such as exaggerating your contribution to the team's report or lying to a friend about why you declined an invitation. On the positive side, finding a wallet and making the effort to return it, or tipping generously when warranted, spreads good habits.

Our principles define us. They tell the world who we are, how we will behave in a given situation, and what we would hope for from others. We don't get to cherry-pick principles based on convenience. And we don't get free passes. Honesty and integrity are just as valid at the supermarket, and with respect to small amounts, as they are with our family, friends, and work colleagues and bigger transgressions.

In the case presented at the beginning of the question, there is no need for additional information. We have money that isn't ours, and we know to whom it belongs.

Finally, while this dilemma may seem to be mostly about you (and possibly the cashier who made the mistake), not so fast. We affect many others over time when we start to negotiate with ourselves in compromising our ethics ("just this once"), instead of sweating the small stuff. Whether it is the cashier, a colleague we disrespect, a partner that we subtly bully, or that friend who is upset about a social media post, our choices always affect others.

Small things matter even when the frequency or the seriousness of the offense are not at issue. As Admiral

McRaven says, and Rob Chesnut's mother modeled, it's about training our ethics muscles and our minds. It's about being honest with ourselves so that we see clearly that there are indeed lines to be drawn. It is about establishing an ethics baseline and building an ethics reflex, so that we can do the big things right. It's about making our ethics bed.

Chapter 2

Politics, Community, and Culture

Should we prosecute someone who steals food during a crisis?

A student once described to me witnessing a young teenager grab a bag of chips from a New York subway vendor and run off without paying. He could have reported the incident to the police or the vendor . . . or walked away and forgotten the matter. Instead, he paid for the chips. He didn't know whether this grab-and-run was a one-off in response to a dare, a pattern of minor theft, or the desperate act of a starving youth. So my student responded with compassion and generosity—and deft creativity.

Now let's up the ante—examining widespread food theft during a crisis. On August 29, 2005, Hurricane Katrina tore through coastal Louisiana, breaching the levees around New Orleans. Hundreds of thousands of people were evacuated; about 25,000 of those left behind fled to the Superdome. Approximately 80 percent of New Orleans was underwater. There was almost no food, shelter, or potable water. Almost 2,000 lives were lost as a result of engineering flaws and ineffective governmental oversight.

With $108 billion in damages, it was at the time one of the costliest hurricanes in U.S. history.

In the days that followed the media reported that "looters floated garbage cans filled with clothing and jewelry down the street" or stole drinks, chips, and diapers from a Walgreens drugstore. Citizens who never would have imagined themselves stealing were driven to take food out of necessity.

Police responses were inconsistent. Some police stood guard to allow stealing for necessities; other looters were arrested—a jail was constructed of chain-link cages in the main New Orleans train station.

Exploration

This story cuts to the core of our humanity. Watching the news, I felt overwhelming sympathy for the victims of Katrina. I also felt a foreboding that a major disaster could cause such damage to our infrastructure, shatter the lives of so many citizens, and result in further inequality in the aftermath. I found myself thinking, What would I have done if *my* children were desperate for food or water? What would happen if the most well-intended members of the National Guard and my local police were unable to protect us? For me, the primary principles in a crisis like this are human safety and well-being—but tightly tethered to dignity, independence, and compassion.

The two principles of safety and well-being are hard to argue with even if breaking the law is the trade-off. We can pay back stolen goods or broken windows (and sometimes shop owners can collect insurance or government support). But we can't walk back the consequences of not having enough money to pay for health care, hospitalization, shelter, or food. Who among us wouldn't consider grabbing food we couldn't pay for if our child was starving? Who among us wouldn't be grateful for someone looking the other way in a time of crisis?

In stark contrast, looting is unethical, whatever is going on in the streets, and whether the perpetrator is in a gang, a mother of six, a protester, or a police officer.

Clear principles can help us combat *arbitrariness* that can occur in times of crisis—one of the most dangerous drivers of the spread of unethical behavior (whether the unfair distribution of ventilators during the Covid-19 crisis or ignoring the poorest neighborhoods post-Katrina). Arbitrariness conveys the message that there is no clear link between our efforts and our impact—so why bother to try? Arbitrariness on the part of even highly skilled and well-meaning authorities also matters, such as instances of some New Orleans police enforcing the law while some overlooked it.

The people who looted or committed violent acts out of pent-up anger against the authorities hurt fellow citizens who had nothing to do with the inequality of the disaster response, or decades of poverty. (In my view the disproportionately negative impact of this disaster on poorer communities is not random: it's the toxic mix of systemic and institutionalized racism and inequality.)

Whatever your view on prosecuting first-time offenders,

consider how we, as individuals and as a society, can ethically respond to such crises with principles, and to avoid arbitrariness.

No one should have to choose between stealing food and going hungry. My fallback position is that when theft of food and necessities for survival is the only option, we should show respect and compassion and redouble our efforts to contribute to healing.

Do we have a responsibility to speak up if we're in a conversation where racist comments are made?

Imagine that you are at an after-hours business event with other people from your industry, and while circulating around the room over drinks and hors d'oeuvres someone makes a racist remark. You are not part of the conversation; you are a bystander. You don't know the individual well, but you recognize what company they work for. You are wondering if you have an obligation to speak up—or if you even want to speak up. This has happened to you before with complete strangers, like when striking up a casual conversation with the person in front of you while waiting in line to buy a coffee. What would you do?

Exploration

Racism plagues our society. I attempt to approach questions relating to discrimination, inequality, and injustice with a hefty dose of humility, as well as gratitude for my many teachers. I include friends, colleagues, and students who have modeled thoughtfulness and sensitivity, as well as the insights of writers such as James Baldwin, Maya Angelou, Ta-Nehisi Coates, Toni Morrison, Claudia Rankine, and Ibram X. Kendi.

Racism is never acceptable. However, confronting racism asks us to consider when and under what circumstances we speak up. If we say nothing, we are complicit. Passively standing by results in impunity (the person getting away with racist comments, or worse, assuming their views and language are acceptable, or at least tolerated). Impunity is one of the most dangerous drivers of the spread of unethical behavior because it sends the message to observers that they, too, can get away with the unacceptable attitudes and language. We are never really a bystander to racism. By hearing the language, we become a participant. We are not responsible for the other person's behavior, but we are responsible for our response to it.

First, ask *why* you should (or shouldn't) speak up in a specific situation. The goal should be to stop racist rhetoric and the misguided ideas that underpin them, rather than bringing attention to yourself or stirring up trouble.

Next, ask *how* you can best speak up. Are you explaining, with humility and respect, why the words make you uncomfortable and why you feel we can't tolerate racism in any guise? Or do you attempt to call the person out, embarrassing them and upping the ante? There are many ways to speak up effectively. In all circumstances, it starts with listening well, paying attention, and aligning your words with these goals. You can speak up at the time, and also have a private conversation later, write a thoughtful text or email, or even send the person an article or book that has helped you along your own journey. If you encounter racism at work, I strongly advise reporting it to Human Resources, your boss, a confidential hotline, or Ombuds services.

I tell my students that they should never miss an opportunity to shout out someone else's positive contributions to human dignity, but decline every opportunity to call out someone else's error or weakness. To me, racism is a clear exception. *Call it out.* But offer the benefit of the doubt; share your point of view rather than casting shame and blame; learn along with the person you are correcting. Gratuitous criticism and "gotcha" retorts make *you* the ethics problem, rather than the other person's racist behavior or words.

Some people don't speak up out of understandable concern of saying the wrong thing or initiating a confrontation. Sometimes, the offender is in a position of power and we fear retaliation. Other times, we freeze and lose the moment to shock, outrage, or inaction. But in the words of bestselling author Ibram X. Kendi, the director of the Center for Antiracist Research at Boston University, we are either actively antiracist, or racist; there's no such thing as neutrality. We must be active participants in combating racism in all its forms.

Should voting be mandatory?

Compulsory or mandatory voting is a system in which eligible citizens are legally required to register and vote, and may suffer penalties, sanctions, or fines if they fail to do so.

More than twenty countries have mandatory voting requirements, including Argentina, Australia, Belgium, Costa Rica, and Mexico—although violations are not always enforced. Before Australia passed mandatory voting for national elections in 1924, only 47 percent of registered voters participated in the national election. Over 91 percent of registered voters voted in Australia's 2019 federal election.

Historically, voter turnout in U.S. general elections has been low. In the 2016 presidential election, only 55 percent of eligible voters cast a ballot. (In 2020, voting was the highest it's been in a century, with an estimated 66.8 percent of voters voting.) In addition, voting is often disincentivized, depending on the laws of the individual states that set the voting rules, and many voters experience disenfranchisement. In 2021, Georgia passed a slew of laws that many argue discourage voting by minorities, requiring photo IDs, encouraging or discouraging voting by mail, and limiting the number and location of polling places, which leads to long lines. Florida and Texas have passed similar voting laws. Add to this mix the overwhelming challenge of verifying the accuracy of the information the public receives, including fake news on social media, microtargeted advertising, and potential influence by foreign agents.

Exploration

I believe that with the right to vote—an immense privilege—also comes great responsibility. Our vote, or decision not to vote, impacts the outcomes of elections, and speaks not only to how we view ethics, but positively or negatively affects ethics in the political sphere.

Advocates of mandatory voting focus on our collective civic duty, similar to paying taxes or obeying the speed limit. Some experts argue that it sends a message to the public that everyone's voice is valued and could stimulate more engagement in the issues of the day. In the short term, mandatory voting might do away with the potential misuse of voter ID requirements, or the politically motivated distribution of polling locations or ballot boxes to limit access. If *everyone* is required to vote, disenfranchisement becomes harder to accomplish.

Critics, on the other hand, argue that mandatory voting diminishes individual freedom, including the decision *not* to use one's voice. Inaction is also a form of action, and citizens may choose to use their voice by *not* speaking. Some critics also argue that forcing citizens to vote could lead to box ticking—citizens voting without informing themselves about the candidates and issues—or even the deliberate manipulation of the vote. Some are skeptical that an effective system can be put in place that doesn't exacerbate inequality through penalties that fall most heavily on those with the fewest resources.

Ultimately, the most important question is whether mandatory voting protects or undermines democracy.

To get our bearings, consider other constitutionally entrenched rights, such as freedom of speech and freedom to assemble, which allow us, but do not force us, to speak or assemble peacefully.

Also, ask whether the decision *not to vote* harms others. The potential consequences for others are fundamental to laws about drunk driving, wearing seatbelts, and smoking in public places (jail time, losing a driver's license, fines). Does abstaining from voting harm others? If so, what sanctions would be appropriate to spur compliance and mitigate that harm?

Instead of falling back on a "yes or no" answer, we should consider blended solutions and alternatives. With or without mandatory voting, we should ensure that every citizen has not just the right, but the *opportunity* to vote. We should make registration and voting easier. We should create incentives to vote: time off work, offering a tax credit or voucher for those who vote, and improving communication about the candidates and issues. We should develop technology to assure tamper-proof ways to vote by smartphone. We could also strengthen warnings of the dangers of not voting—the "smoking kills" version for civic responsibility.

We should only consider adopting compulsory voting if we can't find another way to overcome low voter turnout and barriers to voting that don't effectively take choice away from citizens. And there should be exemptions to the requirement where appropriate, such as religious exemptions.

With or without mandatory voting, every vote matters. The I VOTED stickers are a hopeful sign that many of us are proud to vote, and to let others know that we did. Would we have the same impetus to wear a sticker that said, essentially, THEY MADE ME VOTE?

Should we give money directly to those who are experiencing homelessness?

E very time I walk by the local Peet's Coffee shop in my northern California town, a homeless man outside extends a cup as a way of asking for money. We exchange greetings and smiles, and I often do drop some money for breakfast into his cup. I see him so often that he recognizes me. One block over, the local boutique grocery store prominently displays a sandwich board pleading with customers not to give to individuals asking for money, but rather to donate to nonprofit organizations set up to support those in need.

If you live in a major metropolitan area, it's likely that you frequently encounter someone experiencing homelessness (although homelessness is not by any means confined to large cities). In *The 2020 Annual Homeless Assessment Report to Congress*, the U.S. Department of Housing and Urban Development reported that 580,000 people experienced homelessness on any given night in the U.S.

Exploration

This is what I refer to as an "ethics on the fly" question—one we can answer with the limited information we already have at hand. I don't think anyone wants to live on the street, sleeping all night in the cold or begging for change to buy food. Most of us don't know what it's like to sleep on a sidewalk or subway grate for days, weeks, or months, never knowing where our next meal is coming from, living a life of fear, stigma, and sheer physical discomfort. As someone close to me once said, you don't know what poverty is like until you're going through it, with no clear path of escape. In addressing this question, I would lead with compassion, dignity, autonomy, generosity, and respect.

People end up experiencing homelessness and hunger for many reasons that have nothing to do with unethical behavior or criminal intent. One recipient of assistance from a nonprofit I worked for, a father with a successful job and loving family, was walking his young daughter to school one day when a taxicab hit and killed her. He subsequently experienced mental illness and drug addiction, ultimately losing his job and his ability to support himself. According to a 2021 study in high-income countries, approximately three quarters of the people experiencing homelessness also experience a mental health disorder.

When I do choose to give, I offer cash rather than food. It's not my job to second-guess what the person might do with the money I give them. To me, giving them the dignity to make their own choices is the least I can offer. I also give them information, when it's appropriate and they are interested, about other services—a food bank, shelter, nonprofit, or mental health organization—that can provide additional aid. You may feel differently, and wish to ensure that your generosity is being spent on food rather than alcohol, cigarettes, or drugs.

We don't owe any particular person or organization our generosity. But we can lift our gaze and contribute in whatever way makes the most sense to us (whether giving our time, money, used clothing, a smile, or an offer to babysit while someone goes to a job interview). We can also support organizations that aid those experiencing homelessness, and fight to change the system that allows people to go hungry, without shelter, and without basic medical care in one of the wealthiest countries in the world.

What are the key ethical considerations behind museums returning artifacts to the countries of origin?

In 1897, James Phillips, a British government official, went to visit the ruler of the Kingdom of Benin, in what is now Nigeria. When Phillips and most of his party were killed, the British government sent in 1,200 troops who ransacked the palace in retaliation, taking troves of valuable items. Over the decades, at least 3,000 of the Benin Bronzes (as they became known)—artifacts from the thirteenth to the seventeenth centuries—were dispersed throughout the world to museums and private collections. Almost 1,000 sculptures are on display and in storage in the vaults of the British Museum. The governments of both Nigeria and Benin City have sought to have the artifacts returned, but museums are unclear as to whom the art should be returned, or where it would be housed—a planned museum in Benin City is an empty lot today.

French president Emmanuel Macron promised that France would return twenty-six of the stolen artifacts (a small percentage of the works requested by the government of Benin). In 2021, the Netherlands announced it would begin "returning cultural heritage objects to their country of origin." "There is no place in the Dutch State collection for cultural heritage objects that were acquired by theft," said Ingrid van Engelshoven, the Netherlands' minister of education, culture, and science. And the Metropolitan Museum of Art has had to reassess the provenance of many pieces in its collection, including an artifact known as Nedjemankh and His Gilded Coffin, which the Met returned to Egypt in 2019.

Exploration

The starting point for this question is for both the museums and the countries of origin to work together to protect irreplaceable historic objects—whatever the national origin or current political context. Preservation is paramount in determining location, transporting, display, and storage—including whether objects are susceptible to theft or terrorism. Independent experts and home country experts should review museums' claims that objects cannot be safely transported or maintained in their home country.

Countries able to contribute to the protection of artifacts should do so, regardless of the rightful ownership or the location of the artifacts. (Private donors support such efforts outside their own countries as with the restoration of Venice.)

In terms of legal ownership, I believe robust peer-reviewed scholarship and outside expertise (ideally a diverse international group) should determine provenance and inform rightful ownership. Museums, plus governments and the public, must confront the range of possible broken links in the chain—theft during colonial rule, wartime looting, illegally purchased pieces hidden away in private collections, and more.

The accessibility of art and artifacts is another thorny factor, since cultural heritage should be accessible to all. Some argue that in major metropolitan cities like New York, London, Paris, and Madrid, more people will see them. That may be true, but if the art originated in West Africa, it is not likely that many West African citizens would see it. Covid-19 travel restrictions—not to mention violence from terrorism and political unrest—complicate equitable access. Many artifacts can travel on loan, unlike ancient architecture sites such as the Taj Mahal in India, the pyramids of Egypt, or the Great Wall of China. And technology can bring us closer. Google Arts & Culture and many other online sources offer online tours, education, and interaction.

So how do museum administrators navigate these potentially conflicting ethical principles? Let's first separate the question of ownership from location. Museums regularly house and display collections that they have on loan. Loans of artwork can be renewed indefinitely. Conceding that Greece owns the Elgin Marbles in the British Museum or that present-day Nigeria owns the Benin Bronzes does not necessarily mean that rightful ownership cannot be recognized while allowing them to remain *on loan* to a European or American museum.

Second, we should heed the global call to decolonialize,

to free our countries from colonial attitudes. Holding on to another country's property is a form of colonization—and failure to stand up to past moral failings. We should take responsibility for restoring justice, without jeopardizing any artifacts. Hopefully France's and the Netherlands' commitment to returning stolen artwork will prove contagious.

Museums all over the world depend on revenue from collections and donors, as well as on government support. And local and national governments depend on artifacts for tourism revenue. While a museum's finances shouldn't be central to the decision, I want to be realistic. Organizations should integrate ethics into their budgets. Museums and governments that borrow, lend, or claim to own artifacts should heed the research and ethical concerns and manage the financial consequences accordingly.

How should we engage with the works of artists, writers, producers, and actors who commit sexual misconduct?

In the two-part 2019 HBO documentary *Leaving Neverland*, two men describe being invited to pop star Michael Jackson's Neverland Ranch as young boys and allege that while they were there Jackson showed them pornographic images and molested them. Jackson's album *Thriller* is one of the bestselling albums of all time.

Despite allegations against him, and although he was indicted in 2003 on ten criminal counts, including child molestation, Michael Jackson was never convicted. Hollywood producer Harvey Weinstein was convicted of sexual assault and rape and sentenced to twenty-three years in prison in March 2020. And R & B musician R. Kelly was convicted of nine counts that included eight violations of the Mann Act against sexual trafficking in September 2021. The allegations prompted long-overdue conversations about how we should engage with the work of artists accused of such behavior.

Exploration

Sexual misconduct of all kinds is abhorrent and unacceptable. When famous artists are perpetrators, how we react individually and as a society reflects on *our own* ethics.

With the question of whether and under what circumstances we would seek to restrict or ban someone's artistic legacy, it is important to identify the stakeholders. In the cases of Michael Jackson and R. Kelly, the stakeholders include all of us who listen to their music on Spotify, Apple Music, and other streaming services; the directors of their shows and videos; and those involved in their tours and beyond. With Harvey Weinstein, the stakeholders include all of us who have watched his films over the decades, as well as innocent artists and contributors to the creation of those films.

If we choose to urge theaters and streaming services like Netflix and Amazon Prime Video to no longer show or carry or stream the work of these artists, we should keep in mind that banning artistic material negates the work and contributions of many other artists and contributors who did nothing wrong. Such bans would also distort the artistic canon and deprive future audiences of enjoying the art and understanding the full sweep of art history.

For these reasons, without in any way tolerating their despicable behavior, I lean toward protecting the art that Michael Jackson, Harvey Weinstein, and R. Kelly created. Eradicating an individual's oeuvre does little to discourage other predators. It also does not penalize those around them who tolerated their behavior and did not step forward. Most importantly, it does not repair the trauma and suffering that survivors experience.

Then the question becomes, what *should* we do, knowing that nothing can make up for the survivors' unspeakable suffering? Each of us must probe whether our own response is consistent with our principles. We can decide individually whether and how we want to engage with the art of those who have committed sexual misconduct. As a society, we can fight to ensure that the artists (or their estate) lose rights to future profits, as well as any copyrights they hold. The distributors of Harvey Weinstein's films could add a note to the beginning of his films that he was convicted of felony sex crimes, and that the participants in the creation of the film do not condone such behavior. While an imperfect solution, by removing financial gain, reminding everyone of the specifics of the horrific behavior, and providing an educational opportunity, I believe we show respect for art, music, history, cinema, and the many stakeholders involved in creating that art, while putting it in its factual context.

These very small steps toward showing respect for the survivors might at least assure them that their truth will not be covered up or forgotten. And truth would also be the essential first step if a perpetrator seeks to take responsibility for their despicable acts and commit to change.

Should there be age limits for U.S. presidential candidates?

At age seventy-eight, former U.S. vice president Joe Biden was the oldest person to be sworn in as president of the United States. His opponent, President Donald Trump, was seventy-four at the time of his reelection campaign. For perspective, the youngest U.S. president was John F. Kennedy, who was forty-three on inauguration day; President Emmanuel Macron of France, at age thirty-nine upon taking office, is the youngest French president in history; and New Zealand prime minister Jacinda Ardern became the world's youngest leader at thirty-seven. U.S. presidential candidates must be natural-born citizens, at least thirty-five years of age, and have been a resident for fourteen years, as spelled out in the Constitution. In the U.S., it is left for the voters to determine if a candidate or political leader is fit to be elected to office. Unfortunately, voters may not know a great deal about the health of those seeking the presidency. Neither the Democratic frontrunners nor President Trump released full health records in 2020, although many released some medical documents and letters from their physicians testifying to their overall health.

This question could apply just as easily to U.S. senators, members of the House of Representatives, and the Supreme Court. Most recently, legendary Supreme Court justice Ruth Bader Ginsburg passed away at eighty-seven having served for decades through multiple illnesses.

Exploration

Two questions target the ethics of presidential age limits. First, the information we need: do age limits help assure us that the president is fit to act on behalf of the nation in accordance with an individual voter's—and our nation's—ideals? Some argue that with age comes greater wisdom. Others believe that older presidents in their eighth decade and beyond might not have the physical stamina and mental acuity to handle highly complex, life-and-death decisions.

Second, do age limits violate our nation's principles? To some, imposing a maximum age limit on candidates would thwart democracy and violate free speech, as voters would be prevented from electing the candidate they prefer. Generalizing about the impact of age on an individual's physical stamina and mental acuity could be inaccurate and discriminatory.

For perspective, let's consider a few other professions that include an age limit when there is a responsibility for human life or significant social impact. At one hospital I advise, mandatory retirement for surgeons is usually set at age sixty-eight, while the age for nonsurgical doctors requiring less dexterity is seventy. Under the Age Discrimination in Employment Act of

1967, companies are permitted to impose mandatory retirement for executives in high policy positions at age sixty-five. The mandatory retirement age for commercial airline pilots is sixty-five. The mandatory retirement age for military personnel under the rank of general or admiral is sixty-two.

The president is the ultimate decision maker in terms of responsibility for both human life (most notably as commander in chief of the U.S. Armed Forces) and global policy. The election of the president affects a vast stakeholder group, including citizens of other countries who have no say in our elections. The president has the potential to impact virtually every person in the world—as a model of ethics or a spreader of unethical behavior—today and for generations to come. The president helps to influence national policies, the advancement of technology (autonomous weapon systems, nuclear weapons, space exploration), the climate, geopolitical stability, national security, and infrastructure. However, in contrast to some of the professions just mentioned, the president's position, while emotionally and physically demanding, does not require high levels of physical dexterity or strength. He is also advised by experts and a senior cabinet and is held accountable by checks and balances from the two other branches of government.

In the end, I support our freedom to choose the right person with the right policies and ethics rather than the right age. But it's not "yes or no." We shouldn't prohibit candidates from running for office on the basis of a number, but the information related to each candidate is necessary to assess their leadership capacity and avoid discriminatory generalizations regardless of the number.

Should political candidates and initiatives be allowed to accept donations and support from outside the districts, cities, and states in which they're on the ballot?

C rucial runoff elections for Georgia's two U.S. Senate seats were held on January 5, 2021: between Democratic contender Jon Ossoff and Republican incumbent David Perdue and between Democratic challenger Rev. Raphael Warnock and Republican incumbent Kelly Loeffler. The outcome would determine which party would control the U.S. Senate. The race between Ossoff and Perdue would be the most expensive Senate election in American history; between the primaries, general election, and runoff election, the two candidates spent nearly $470 million. The race between Warnock and Loeffler was the second most expensive in history.

According to FiveThirtyEight (the award-winning website owned by ABC News that analyzes polls based on their accuracy, demographics, and voting patterns), 96 percent of the money Democrats raised through their ActBlue online site came from out-of-state donors. And 92 percent of the money raised by Republicans on the WinRed conservative online site was from non-Georgia residents.

Exploration

The issue of Georgia's Senate elections highlights the ethics opportunities and risks when people and organizations outside of a state fund a significant portion of a state's political campaigns.

Current law often permits individuals, political parties, political action committees (or PACs, organizations that raise money to support or defeat political candidates), and other organizations to contribute to candidates outside of the state they live in or are headquartered in. There is a strong argument in favor in the case of federal elected representatives. The president and Congress enact legislation that affects Americans throughout the country—from civil rights and voting rights to health care and infrastructure. In Georgia's case, the Democrats had to win both seats to have enough votes to be able to hold the majority in the Senate.

When the offices are not national, the argument is often less convincing. It's hard to argue for out-of-state money when it comes to governors and state-level legislators and referendums. Why should citizens outside of a district have a say in who represents the people of that district? Politicians in one state may object to money from another state influencing the outcome of their elections and distorting local fundraising efforts.

However, an argument can also be made that state-specific laws often serve as models for bills and legislation in other states. The passage of voter suppression laws in Georgia has encouraged politicians in other states to propose and pass similar legislation. Florida passed a "stand your ground" law in 2005, justifying the use of deadly force when a person believes they are in serious danger, and versions of this self-defense law have since been adopted in numerous states.

What about corporate donations? In 2010, the Supreme Court in the *Citizens United v. FEC* ruling allowed corporations to spend unlimited amounts of money on campaign ads as long as the money is not given directly to a specific candidate or party. This can give corporations outsize influence in elections, which can overwhelm individual voices and contributions. A key argument was that campaign donations constitute free speech.

In my view, we all should pay close attention to Supreme Court justice John Paul Stevens's ninety-page dissent in the case, in which he argues that the law should distinguish between funding from individual constituents and corporations. Justice Stevens emphasized that corporate campaign funds may exert "undue influence on an officeholder's judgment" and "can generate the impression that corporations dominate our democracy." He added that corporations "have no consciences, no beliefs, no feelings, no thoughts . . . They are not themselves members of 'We the People' by whom and for whom our Constitution was established."

Justice Stevens believed that the laws should distinguish between funding from individual constituents and contributions from corporations and out-of-state donors, and argued for an amendment to the Constitution "to create a level playing field." Even if we don't go as far as prohibiting out-of-state donors, Justice Stevens's proposed exclusion of corporate donations might be a helpful middle ground to making sure that the voices of individual citizens are heard, no matter where they live.

Should college basketball athletes be paid?

I n a recent case, *National Collegiate Athletic Association v. Alston*, the Supreme Court unanimously ruled that the National Collegiate Athletic Association, or NCAA, must allow payment of "education-related benefits" (graduate or vocational tuition, internships, and so forth) to college athletes. The Court declined to rule on other forms of compensation, such as salary or payment for image and likeness. The Court disagreed with the NCAA's argument that allowing such payments would blur the lines between amateur and professional sports or would result in a slippery slope to abuse (like giving athletes sports cars under the guise of needing transportation).

The Supreme Court called the NCAA, the organization that governs college sports, a "massive business," citing examples such as its broadcast contract for March Madness for approximately $1.1 billion per year, and the fact that the president of the NCAA earns approximately $4 million per year. For context, universities with the top-rated teams earn millions of dollars a year from student athletes' unpaid performances on the court largely benefiting athletic departments, coaches, and university administrations. The total revenues from college athletics departments in 2019 was $18.9 billion according to the NCAA.

With practices, games, training, and travel, for basketball players at NCAA Division I universities, their sport is a full-time job—not just in season but throughout the year. Teams can spend fifty hours a week training. Often college basketball players are at the peak of their athletic marketability and could potentially earn huge salaries if they played professionally.

On the other hand, universities offer full scholarships to attract top talent, and players are given a national platform and the kind of media attention that can result in lucrative offers from professional teams after graduation. Moreover, the majority of college athletic departments lose money—on average, $16 million a year, reports the *Wall Street Journal*.

Exploration

Those who argue against paying students point out that student athletes are enrolled full-time as students and not as employees of the university. Many basketball players are on scholarship (which is a form of compensation) from their university already. (NCAA rules permit Division I schools to offer thirteen full scholarships to players in the men's basketball program, and fifteen full scholarships to athletes in the women's program.)

Moreover, paying athletes raises questions of fairness and institutional priorities. Students involved in nonathletic extracurricular activities (like serious musical groups or writing for the college newspaper) do not get paid, so why should players on the basketball team be paid? Why shouldn't the financial resources be used in ways that benefit more students? Paying only student athletes in revenue-generating sports like football and basketball, but not those in other sports, would increase inequality in college athletics.

In addition to their education, student athletes are provided with expensive training facilities, experienced coaching, media exposure, and an environment in which they can develop their skills. Athletes hoping to turn professional can enter the NBA draft if they are nineteen and are a season removed from high school, or they can seek work opportunities outside of sports.

Those in favor of paying players argue that athletes in revenue-generating sports like football and basketball are being exploited as cheap labor. For many, college athletics is their best avenue out of their circumstances. College basketball players generate—through ticket sales, television licensing rights, merchandise sales, and corporate sponsorships—significant income for their schools, without sharing in any of the profits. And during their time in college athletics, they risk serious injury that could prematurely end their athletic careers. While many aspire to play professionally after college, the NCAA estimates that in 2019 only 1.2 percent of men's basketball players will make the NBA.

I often urge us to break out of "yes or no" binary decisions. Recent legal changes seem to strike a fair balance.

Twenty-six states, as of 2021, have passed laws allowing college athletes to receive compensation for their names, images, or likenesses, and several additional states passed similar laws slated to go into effect in the next few years. The NCAA announced that it was embracing a temporary set of rules allowing student athletes to receive compensation for their names, images, or likenesses, beginning July 1, 2021. But watch this space. In the Supreme Court's ruling against the NCAA in June 2021, Justice Brett Kavanaugh indicated the court might be interested in going further in a future case. Other states may have more to say.

Should we remove books from bookstores, libraries, internet sales, and reading lists because they are no longer seen as politically correct or culturally acceptable?

Generations of Americans grew up reading Dr. Seuss's *How the Grinch Stole Christmas!*, *Green Eggs and Ham*, and *The Cat in the Hat*. His inventive wordplay and clever rhymes have been an essential part of childhood and have been instrumental in teaching children to read.

On March 2, 2021, Dr. Seuss Enterprises (the company that controls Dr. Seuss's estate) announced that, after consulting with experts and educators, they had decided to stop publishing six of Seuss's books because of their "hurtful and wrong" portrayals of people from other cultures. None were among his bestselling books. Among the six were *And to Think That I Saw It on Mulberry Street* (first published in 1937) and *If I Ran the Zoo* (first published in 1950), both of which display verbal and visual racial stereotypes.

The decision sparked an enormous controversy with Americans across the political spectrum, some who saw this as a positive corrective for racist and xenophobic children's literature, and others who saw the decision as yet another example of what had become known as "cancel culture," in which aspects of our culture are removed, ostracized, or called out as toxic because they don't reflect evolving social attitudes.

In August 2021, I encountered a vivid reminder of this kind of censorship at my weekly outing to my favorite California bookstore, Kepler's Books & Magazines. An unmistakable sign—BANNED BOOKS—was displayed on a table at the entrance to the open-air tent they had set up. It was the bookstore's way of reminding us of the dangers of censorship. The titles, all fiction, were classics of literature, including works by two authors who had won the Nobel Prize in Literature: J. D. Salinger's *The Catcher in the Rye*, Nobel laureate Toni Morrison's *The Bluest Eye*, Aldous Huxley's *Brave New World*, George Orwell's *1984*, Nobel laureate John Steinbeck's *Of Mice and Men*, Harper Lee's *To Kill a Mockingbird*, Maurice Sendak's *Where the Wild Things Are*, and most recently, J. K. Rowling's Harry Potter books.

I picked up copies of all the books I hadn't yet read and went inside.

Exploration

This question forces us to face a key ethical point: Who gets to determine and enforce the ethics of reading material?

Let's clarify at the outset that the decision to stop publishing several books by Dr. Seuss was taken voluntarily by the rights holder itself, rather than by another organization, publisher, school board, retailer, or individual. Accordingly, this is not what is commonly referred to as "cancellation" by another person or organization.

First, there is a compelling argument that children's books should be held to a higher standard than books for adults, because kids don't have the tools to read books critically. Authors of famous children's books have revised their books over concerns about racist content in the past. When it was first published in 1964, *Charlie and the Chocolate Factory* depicted the Oompa-Loompa factory workers as pygmies from Africa. Facing accusations of racism by the NAACP and others, author Roald Dahl reimagined them in a revised 1973 version of the book as fantasy creatures from Loompaland.

Those opposed to removing books that don't meet contemporary standards argue that banning books from curriculums, libraries, and retailers can be a slippery slope. Ten years ago, new editions of Mark Twain's *The Adventures of Huckleberry Finn* had many of the book's racial slurs removed. Nonetheless, in 2019 two New Jersey state lawmakers issued a resolution to remove *Huckleberry Finn* from state schools entirely. This leads us to important questions: How do we avoid trampling on artistic freedom? Are fictional characters depicting racism helpful to show the damage and consequences of racism? Why would we ban earlier works when contemporary works also contain racist, homophobic, and other unacceptable characters? Does erasing this literary history destroy the foundation for learning from past mistakes, and making and monitoring progress?

The question of who gets to make the decision on which books are banned or made unavailable to the public takes on a new dimension in a technological world. After the Dr. Seuss rights holder's decision, eBay immediately delisted the six books from its site. *New York Times* op-ed columnist Ross Douthat wrote that "in a cultural landscape dominated by a few big companies . . . you don't need state censorship for books to swiftly vanish."

Literature is rife with racism, and even well-meaning teachers and parents don't always recognize it. But we should not rely on authors, rights holders, publishers, and distributors of books alone to arbitrate the acceptability of literature in society. The real progress in understanding the complex relationship among fiction, persistent racism, and the need for systemic change to eradicate racism can only come with broader education and our individual commitment to learn to recognize our own responsibility.

Is it ethically acceptable to alter your date of birth so that you appear younger (or older) than you are?

I n 2018, a sixty-nine-year-old Dutchman named Emile Ratelband petitioned a Netherlands court to have the date on his birth certificate changed from March 11, 1949, to March 11, 1969. He claimed that his doctor told him he had the body of a man in his early forties, and that he feels forty-nine. "Why can't I decide my own age?" Ratelband argued. Ratelband's view: the law should be changed to permit individuals to determine their own biological age, in the same way we can change our name and gender. The court disagreed. There are a number of rights and duties related to age, the court pointed out, such as the right to vote and the duty to attend school. Granting the request would cause "all kinds of legal problems," in the view of the court, effectively erasing twenty years of life events.

Exploration

The answer here rests on the single most important force driving ethics: truth. It is the foundation of our society. Truth is based on facts, not beliefs, feelings, or opinions. Compromised truth is *the* most virulent driver of the spread of unethical behavior; it undergirds every other driver of contagion—from arrogance to fake news to efforts to skirt legal compliance.

Age is a verifiable fact. Our date of birth is recorded in formal government records. There are plenty of reasons that people might like to claim to be older or younger, like making themselves appear younger and potentially more appealing on a dating website or feeling that they can better compete against younger candidates in a job market that often prioritizes youth. Some young people want to appear older to purchase alcohol or get into age-restricted bars and clubs. A member of my family, now deceased, lied about her age for decades because as a young woman she seemed destined for spinsterhood, too old to find a husband in her mind (at age twenty-five at the time).

This is not a whimsical question. Chronological facts such as age are the scaffolding for society: rights and privileges such as marriage, civil partnerships, divorce, citizenship, voter registration, driver's licenses, Medicare, Social Security, immigration forms, and an array of official documents all hinge on chronological accuracy. It is also the foundation for social contracts. We can only consent to certain acts such as medical procedures and sexual relationships when above the legally permitted age to do so. And important matters from medical diagnoses to the ability to perform functions safely at work may depend on our age.

We are not entitled to our own truth—to distorting facts in life or on the internet—despite what we encounter on social media. We *are* entitled to our opinions. If someone asks whether we like their dress, our response is an opinion, not a fact—we can keep it to ourselves if we don't like it, or we can compassionately find something positive to say. Ethical decision making hinges on keeping the difference between fact and opinion squarely in mind.

Should athletes be penalized for using legal marijuana?

On June 28, 2021, Sha'Carri Richardson, the American sprinter who won the women's 100-meter race at the U.S. Olympic Team Trials in track and field in Oregon, accepted a suspension of one month after testing positive for marijuana. The suspension voided her victory at the Olympic trials, meaning that she would not be able to compete in Tokyo in July in the 100-meter race (her signature event), even though she was one of the athletes expected to be a star at the Olympics. Although U.S. Track & Field (USTAF)—the national governing body for the sport in the U.S.—had full discretion to give her a slot in the 4x100-meter relay, which was scheduled for after expiration of the thirty-day punitive period, they declined to do so.

Richardson apologized to fans, family, sponsors, and the media. "Don't judge me, because I am human . . . I just happen to run a little faster." A week before the trials, Richardson, who was raised by her grandmother, learned that her biological mother had died, and she said that she fell into an emotional panic, and used the marijuana to calm her emotions. Marijuana is legal in Oregon.

Nicholas Thompson, CEO of the *Atlantic* magazine

and former editor in chief of *Wired*, in discussing Richardson's case said, "Pretty convinced that marijuana is not a 'performance enhancing' drug for a sprinter. Please let Sha'Carri Richardson run in Tokyo." The *Washington Post* editorial board called on USTAF to lobby the World Anti-Doping Agency to change the rules "rather than lend legitimacy to poor policy" by excluding Richardson from the 4x100-meter relay.

Exploration

Where do we draw the line in crafting rules about legal, occasional, and recreational use of marijuana in athletic competitions?

Marijuana is on the list of substances prohibited by the World Anti-Doping Agency, or WADA, and the U.S. Olympic & Paralympic Committee follows its rules. The list, which is extensive, is updated each year. The reason for the ban is that WADA believes marijuana can enhance performance, it poses a health risk to athletes, and its use violates the "spirit of the sport" (including the idea that the "role model of athletes in modern society is intrinsically incompatible with use or abuse of cannabis"). Other banned substances include anabolic androgenic steroids, growth hormones, diuretics, stimulants, and erythropoietins, all of which can enhance performance. However, marijuana is only banned the day before a competition, and a small amount of THC, the main psychoactive substance, will not cause a positive test. The minimum penalty for a positive test, which Richardson received, is a one-month suspension.

Attempts to enhance athletic performance by using banned substances is clearly cheating. But legal recreational use of marijuana is not a performance enhancement, according to the *Journal of Sports Medicine and Physical Fitness* and other experts. In the wake of Richardson's suspension, the *New York Times* reported "an overview of the research concludes that marijuana hinders performance by reducing stamina and peak performance." In 2019, Major League Baseball removed marijuana from its banned substances list effective Spring Training of 2020.

We should also consider the use of substances that are permitted, like alcohol—potentially dangerous to both health and the role model objective, if abused. Some studies suggest that caffeine may enhance athletic endurance. Perhaps because caffeine is contained in so many beverages and products, from coffee, tea, and soda to protein bars, attempting to ban it would be virtually impossible. (To be clear, I'm not arguing that all products containing caffeine should be banned—just that we need perspective.)

By Richardson's own acknowledgment, she knew the rules. We often live by guidelines and ethical standards to be part of a community—for example, a university, a competition, or a workplace—that are more restrictive than the generally applicable laws and rules. Effective international guidelines can spread positive standards and behaviors and raise our ethics along with our athletics.

Richardson should not have done what she did. But she was a role model here in two important respects. She showed us that there is no place for blame and shame in ethics—deploying her world-class athlete status and celebrity to remind us that we all make mistakes instead of offering excuses. And she took responsibility and made a plan to move forward: the very definition of ethical resilience.

WADA and the U.S. Olympic & Paralympic Committee are rightfully committed to eradicating dangerous, performance-enhancing substances. But in my view the issue of banning legal marijuana use is ripe for reconsideration.

Is voting—or deciding not to vote—an ethics choice?

I received an email from BallotTrax Notifications in the fall of 2020: "Your ballot for the 2020 General Election was received and will be counted. Thank you for voting!" The verification of my vote was particularly important to me for a presidential election—it recorded one of the most ethically important decisions that I can make.

In these challenging times, voting—and considering a candidate's ethics in our decisions—can seem daunting. I have several friends who admitted to me before the 2020 U.S. presidential election that they planned to sit it out. They were reacting to the deluge of claims, facts and fake news, and the extreme partisanship. There were many other factors at play as well—wait times, the potential to become infected by Covid-19, and the very real constraints embedded in our voting infrastructure that disenfranchise voters, such as gerrymandering, manipulation of the location of official voting ballot boxes, and challenges to online voting. Particularly in combination, these challenges understandably made voting feel, for some, overwhelming and not worth the effort.

Exploration

The election of a political leader—whether at the federal, state, or local level—is a game-changing opportunity to vote our consciences.

Abstaining from voting diminishes our influence on matters such as national security, domestic policy, individual rights, privacy, Supreme Court appointments, and immigration. We forfeit our voices on cutting-edge, ethically critical issues such as internet safety, gun rights, gene editing, global warming, and artificial intelligence that will shape society for decades to come. And because we have the power to choose—whether or not we use it—we have responsibility; refraining from voting does not absolve us of ethical responsibility for the results of elections.

I work with a four-word framework for ethical decision making that can help guide us through this question: *principles*, *information*, *stakeholders*, and *consequences*.

First, your principles signal to the world who you are, how you act, and how you expect others to behave. Do the candidates' stated principles align with yours?

Second, evaluate the available information. Ask whether the candidates' actions—their behaviors, policies, voting records, and positions on specific issues—align with their stated principles and promises. Conversely, ask whether the candidate exhibits drivers of the spread of unethical behavior: greed, bullying, failure to listen, abuse of power, a demand for loyalty over a diversity of views, arrogance, and manipulation of social media. Most importantly, ask whether the candidate values truth. Compromising truth is, in my view, the greatest global systemic risk of our time, because it infiltrates and catalyzes every other action and behavior.

If you strongly agree with the candidate's policies (or you're a single-issue voter) but find their behavior abhorrent, ask yourself: Would I tolerate this same behavior from a friend? How would I feel if the CEO of my company or my direct boss acted this way?

Finally, think about stakeholders and consequences. Some would argue that your individual vote doesn't matter. But fewer than a combined total of 80,000 votes in the states of Michigan, Wisconsin, and Pennsylvania would have swung the presidential election to Hillary Clinton in 2016. Al Gore lost to George W. Bush in 2000 in the decisive state of Florida by 537 votes out of over 6 million cast. More recently, in the two elections in Georgia for the U.S. Senate, the two Democratic candidates, in a traditionally Republican state, won runoff elections, by about 55,000 votes in the case of Jon Ossoff, and about 93,000 votes in the case of Raphael Warnock, giving Democrats control of the Senate. So not only did these elections affect people on a state level, but also the national level and beyond our borders.

The consequence of abstaining from voting is that we are giving up our power to determine who leads us and the ethics of our leadership today and in the future. One of the candidates is going to be elected. We don't get to choose "none of the above." If all eligible voters vote, and consciously factor in the ethics of the candidates into our decisions, imagine how we would raise the collective ethical standards of the leaders we elect.

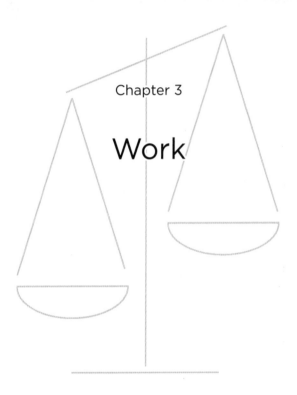

Chapter 3

Work

What is appropriate behavior in a "business social" setting?

The 2018 *Financial Times* headline read: "Men Only: Inside the charity fundraiser where hostesses are put on show." The story that followed described the exclusive Presidents Club Charity Dinner, an annual "secretive black-tie" event at one of London's most prestigious hotel ballrooms, that hired 130 hostesses wearing revealing black outfits and underwear. The charity donated money to the world-renowned Great Ormond Street Hospital for Children, bringing together business colleagues, clients, the political elite, and wealthy donors, in what was supposed to be a social evening. The *Financial Times* reported that "At an after-party many hostesses—some of them students earning extra cash—were groped, sexually harassed and propositioned."

Another example: At a company conference in Texas, which included corporate clients, managers, and employees, the days were full, but the evenings were free. A mid-level female manager casually suggested that her team—all men—go out for drinks at a local strip club.

Exploration

Most work social situations don't make newspaper headlines or involve political leaders. But events that mix business with leisure (and often alcohol) can frequently go awry ethically. And taking a wrong step can alter career trajectories and reputations.

Social gatherings are an important part of work, whether catching up at the coffee machine, formal company events like a holiday party, inviting colleagues to charity events, or more informal smaller group activities. There's nothing unethical about colleagues having a drink or participating in a sporting activity after work. But over the years, I have seen a disproportionate number of high-performing, thoughtful people tainting their reputations in these mixed social settings.

The ethical boundaries between work and our personal lives are not complicated. To understand expectations for behavior at an event described as "business social," just eliminate the word "social" in your mind, and you'll have your guide. Ditto any social situation with colleagues. This includes going out for meals, or an evening out when traveling for work. Conferences are not ethics-free zones—even after hours and off-site. And this applies to all aspects of behavior, from attire and alcohol consumption to topics of conversation. Employees can be made to feel uncomfortable or pressured to participate in various activities, particularly if invited by a manager or boss. Nonetheless we are each responsible for our behavior, whether or not a manager invited us.

Headlines about misconduct at Uber, the Presidents Club event, and beyond have effectively put organizations on notice that wherever misbehavior happens (even online) the world no longer tolerates a culture of "it's not that serious." Let's be clear: there is no corporate "culture" that should tolerate inappropriate language or behavior in the office, online, or around gatherings of company stakeholders outside of the office. And in the end, corporate culture reflects individual decisions.

Every CEO and chief legal, ethics, or compliance officer I know has seen the destructive fallout of drinking too much. People say and do things they never otherwise would. Rob Chesnut, former chief ethics officer of Airbnb, described what he called Rob's Rule to me: two drinks. That's his maximum, to have a nice time and remain in control. Your own rule may be different. But as Rob says, the point is to have a rule in place before you start socializing. The worst time to negotiate that kind of stop limit with yourself is while you're at a party.

A lot of reported misbehavior occurs at after-parties. Here again, there is no problem with colleagues going off as a group to a bar or a restaurant after the formal event. But in a business setting, drop the word "after"; behave as if the original business event is continuing. The ethics haven't changed, whether the partners are there or not.

Overstepping boundaries or outright misconduct is not limited to a particular gender or level of seniority. Companies are responsible for clarifying policies and consequences. But it bears repeating that each of us is responsible for our actions.

Should your employer have a say in what you post on your private social media?

A key member of the senior management team of a company posted anti–Black Lives Matter movement comments on her private social media account. Offended by the posts, a group of employees wanted the CEO to fire the executive.

In practice, the individual involved was one of the company's strongest proponents of diversity and inclusion and ran a highly diverse team. She took issue with the politics of a splinter group within the movement, not with the importance of fighting racism. The CEO asked the executive to take down the social media posting and apologize. The executive refused, citing her freedom to post on private social media as long as the posts are in accordance with the law and the social media company's terms of service.

Exploration

People chatting about the inner workings of a company or current events used to be called watercooler gossip. The audience reach was limited and the banter by and large reasonably acceptable.

Today, millions share their personal lives and political views on multiple social media and communications platforms, from Facebook and Twitter to Instagram, Slack, and LinkedIn. Furthermore, companies depend on social media to reach customers and promote products. With some companies, the platform *is* their business model. Drawing a line between work life and private life can pit free speech against a company's right to uphold its ethical principles—and protect its reputation.

Four guides apply in all situations.

First, inciting violence, hate speech, bullying, and harassment is off limits (and also not permitted under the terms of service of most social media apps).

Second, you may not have control over where content ends up. Anything you post could be forwarded to employers, clients, the media, and beyond. When in doubt, err on the side of professionalism.

With company communications, there are some clear "no" situations. Company electronic signature lines (with titles and work contact details), email addresses, stationery, websites, and logos are for company business only. You are acting as a representative of the company. What would you think if colleagues were to advocate for causes or products you or others don't support using company communications?

Private social media is a more challenging dilemma. For example, sexually graphic material or offensive jokes are often within the normal bounds of free speech, but not likely acceptable to an employer. What you do outside of work also reflects who you are as a person, as well as your judgment. Ask yourself if you are potentially making others feel uncomfortable, or even undermining trust—and how private your social media groups are. In the above scenario, the executive could have communicated privately her specific concerns about the behaviors and statements of individuals within the Black Lives Matter movement, while recognizing the movement's important anti-racist work and affirming her commitment to fighting racism at and outside of work. Senior leaders are more visible and have a greater responsibility to a wide range of stakeholders.

Third, the fact that we work from home is not a license to mix the personal with our professional responsibilities. The shift to working remotely due to Covid-19 and new technologies may further smudge the lines. And the boundaries may differ depending on the type of organization you work for (a tech start-up versus a governmental department).

Finally, in some countries, social media can put others in danger. Employees in one situation I researched knew that posting commentary critical of the government was likely to incite a serious response from the police such as arrest. The posting could have been potentially dangerous, whether or not it would have been considered protected speech elsewhere.

Ask yourself whether your post is worth the various risks.

What would you do when others take credit for your work?

As a very junior lawyer, I was working on a huge international deal with a senior associate who was trying to make partner. I spent days preparing over eighty documents for a deal closing. On the morning of the closing, I overheard one of the firm's senior partners complimenting the senior associate I was working with on what he referred to as the "superb organization." She thanked him, slipping in that she had worked through the night, even though I was the one who had stayed up all night to organize the documents.

Exploration

Taking credit when you do not deserve it tramples on ethical principles many of us share: honesty, integrity, collegiality, accountability, generosity, and, most importantly, truth. These principles apply regardless of seniority, or the situation.

Taking credit for other people's work is all too common. For example, the husband of a friend who has a skewed view of his contributions to the evening's dinner, or a colleague accepting a boss's compliment for a report that was largely produced by an outside advisor. Even if these situations seem small, each requires us to tackle the *spread* of unethical behavior, not just the behavior itself. Silence can allow falsity to fester and become the norm. And if we allow truth to be compromised, other threats to ethics will breed as well: competition, jealousy, greed, pressure, fear.

We usually don't need a lot of information to make an ethical decision in scenarios like these. But it's worth considering frequency (whether this is a first offense or a consistent pattern) and the nature of your relationship with the other person (regular interaction versus one-time collaboration). It's also helpful to remember that unconscious bias can sneakily alter our perceptions of who did what—and how much we contributed. Research by Harvard University professor Max H. Bazerman and others shows that when group members are asked what percentage of the group's work was done by each of them, the total "typically far exceeds 100 percent."

How do we respond? Publicly embarrassing the person or involving too many other people is neither helpful, nor a show of the principles listed above. If it's a minor first-time offense with no important consequences, consider yourself on alert and think about acting only if there is a second offense. You might speak to the person, and give them a chance to explain, apologize, and take responsibility (or even correct the misunderstanding). If it's a more serious issue, you can speak to your boss, Human

Resources, another senior person, or an Ombuds service. Or you might sidestep it: armed with confidence in your own contributions, ask for more responsibilities and prove yourself with another assignment.

Do create space for others to grant credit. I ask my Stanford students to report team members' exceptional work after team projects are completed. If you're tempted to accept undue credit by not correcting someone else's assumption, consider the impact on your reputation—the undermining of trust and relationships, not to mention how it might affect your performance evaluations and subsequent recommendations for promotions. And what do you do when your boss asks you to complete a similar task, but you don't really have the skills? That is the danger of contagion of unethical behavior; accepting credit for someone else's work sets a number of ethical violations in motion—the ramifications of which can be hard to foresee.

How would you respond if you witnessed a boss sexually harassing or bullying a more junior colleague?

At the company you work for, you notice some uncomfortable behavior on the part of a manager. At staff meetings, he ignores a female coworker who tries to ask a question. When someone else invites the woman to speak, the manager interrupts, drowning her out. A week later, you overhear him berating the employee at her desk, using inappropriate language. You ask her about it later, but she refuses to talk.

You are a bystander—someone who witnessed bullying and harassment but is not personally involved.

Exploration

As an ethics advisor, I encounter stories of bullying and harassment in organizations of all sizes and with all combinations of seniority.

Bullying often falls on a spectrum, with irritating banter at one end, and sexually or racially charged behavior at the other. Two hallmarks of bullying are the repetition and the targeting of an individual or group. The behavior may range from subtle verbal digs, "accidentally" omitting someone from an email chain, or sabotaging one's ability to do their job—to blatant disrespect or aggression. The tricky cases to resolve are those that are not explicit enough to trigger the company's antibullying policy and don't involve racist or sexual content. Regardless, all types of bullying and harassment are unacceptable.

First, check your company's policy to determine if you have a responsibility to intervene, regardless of whether you are a manager. It may also indicate if you are protected from potential retaliation and offer guidance on whether the behavior you witnessed is bullying, harassment, or sexual misconduct. To me, safety and respect are the most important considerations in this situation. If a colleague's safety or well-being is at stake, I would consider intervening early and quickly.

One potential consequence of not taking action is the continuation or even escalation of the behavior. If the manager's actions are not investigated, your colleague will continue to suffer, potentially undermining trust in the organization. Others may begin to see the manager's behavior as normal, or even copy it to curry favor.

If your colleague declines having you act on her behalf, perhaps she would agree to your sharing just one aspect of the behavior. Or if the manager's actions make you and others uncomfortable, you might consider reporting the impact of the behavior on you, or joining others in reporting it. Consider consulting with a confidential source—your

Human Resources manager, an Ombuds service, an external lawyer, or your own manager. And you can continue to show understanding and support to your colleague and be available to step in if she changes her mind.

Bystander scenarios can occur anywhere: on the street, at the gym, at the movies. Certain situations require immediate action, such as calling the police if someone is in physical danger. (That said, you have no obligation to put yourself in harm's way by intervening directly.) In the workplace, you are operating within a structure in which you are *automatically involved—a stakeholder*. You have company regulations and guidelines to help you; you are more likely to be personally affected by the behavior and require protection from retaliation.

Reporting the abuse could result in conflict with your colleague if she doesn't want your involvement and feels you are disrespecting her privacy. And I would be remiss in not acknowledging that taking action could result in retaliation against you or your coworkers by the person accused and those who support them. None of us want to cause more harm by trying to help. Unfortunately, there are no guarantees in this situation.

Should CEOs speak out about important social and political issues of the day?

In March 2021, CEOs from over one hundred companies, including major airlines, retailers, and manufacturers, gathered to discuss taking action against restrictive voting laws that had been enacted in Georgia and were being considered in several states. Kenneth Chenault, former CEO of American Express, and Kenneth Frazier, then CEO of Merck & Co., led an effort to organize seventy-two Black business leaders to sign a letter to band together to fight restrictive voting rights in Georgia and forty-two other states. Delta CEO Ed Bastian called the Georgia voting bill "unacceptable." Alfredo Rivera, the president of North America for Coca-Cola, which is headquartered in Georgia, also spoke out over the new laws, as did Apple CEO Tim Cook. Major League Baseball moved the Draft and the All-Star Game from Atlanta on April 2, 2021, in response to the new voting laws. In contrast, after considerable thought, McDonald's CEO Chris Kempczinski did not speak out against restrictive voting laws. He said, "In the case of voting rights, it wasn't our business. It wasn't aligned with one of our leadership platforms. And we didn't feel like our voice was going to be particularly helpful to addressing the issues."

Senate minority leader Mitch McConnell denounced such efforts, urging corporate leaders to "stay out of politics."

Exploration

While this question might seem just for corporate CEOs and boards, it's one for all of us to consider as employees, consumers, citizens, shareholders, and other stakeholders, about some of the most critical issues affecting society today—and the role and influence business has in these issues and our lives.

CEOs are free to choose what societal issues they speak up about. Importantly, in contrast, CEOs have an *obligation* to speak up about issues clearly within the company's responsibility, like product safety, customer data privacy, or antitrust regulation. In addition, every CEO I know of feels an ethical and legal responsibility to combat racism and other forms of bias and discrimination within their organization (including requiring suppliers, service providers, and other stakeholders to comply with their antidiscrimination policies), and they would owe transparency about any serious misconduct.

When speaking out about societal issues, I recommend CEOs advocate for an organization's lasting principles rather than supporting social movements (in favor of sustainability rather than to promote a particular group or hashtag). Movements can take unpredictable directions, create reputational risk on social media (or worse), and have rogue actors or splinter groups. CEOs should communicate the company's actions to further its principles, while acknowledging mistakes and the work still to be done.

Some CEOs may decide to establish a "no go" zone. For example, multinational companies might take the view that they never speak out to promote or critique a government's political stance—whether authoritarian regimes or democracies. Such blanket bans help leadership to sidestep government requests, and potentially threats, especially to the safety of employees.

Many CEOs stick exclusively to issues that directly affect their business. Kempczinski said in an interview in the *New York Times*, "Where do we speak up on an issue? . . . Is it either directly in our industry . . . or does it go specifically to the pillars that we've said are going to matter to us? So we've talked about jobs and opportunity. We've talked about helping communities in crisis."

Once a CEO has spoken, he or she has started a conversation. Often pressure mounts to continue to speak out or monitor and act on the issue as it evolves. Critics may query why a CEO spoke out on one issue but isn't speaking out on the issue they care most about—like the 145 CEOs who sent Congress a letter demanding action on gun control in 2019, but may not have said anything publicly about the U.S. southern border crisis. No CEO owes us to speak out on our issues or to agree with our views. They do owe us and society to *behave and run their business ethically*.

Would you hire someone who has made a mistake and is looking for a second chance?

I find in my ethics advisory work that organizations are beginning to integrate ethics into the recruiting process: verifying records and behavior, checking social media history, probing references, hiring me to do special ethics-focused interviews. Some job descriptions now highlight a track record of ethical behavior as a necessary qualification. Global organizations take extra care with references to ensure cultural sensitivity. Whether explicitly or not, the attitude is often zero tolerance: past offenders need not apply.

In our personal lives, too, our ethics antennae are up with respect to babysitters, music teachers, and school sports coaches who will interact with our children, and even painters, plumbers, electricians, and other service providers who will be working in our homes.

Exploration

To begin, a few key assumptions: We're not talking about minor offenses, like swiping a pack of gum when we were ten years old. Nor are we talking about the other extreme, like sex offenders or violent criminals whose postprison rights may be a matter of law. We're in the space in between, in which ethics really matter, but the law doesn't offer guidance.

The point here is not forgiveness. We were not the ones harmed by their earlier conduct. And we don't owe anyone a job or a second chance. But here are a few questions that bring considerations such as nonjudgment, compassion, and generosity into practice to help us determine if we are willing to try.

The first question to ask is, Who is this person *today*? You need in-depth information about the precise nature of both the misbehavior and the person's efforts to remedy that behavior and demonstrate permanent change. Ask yourself if the incident was a one-off (a one-time misstatement to save face), or if there is evidence of a pattern of misbehavior (repeatedly posting hate speech on social media). Check whether they have guardrails in place to ensure they don't slip again. The more time that has passed without further incidents, the more credibility they have.

Next, look outward. Has the world changed? Many women in my mother's generation smoked while pregnant because in 1960 no one knew any better. People's attitudes and beliefs about racism, sexism, and LGBTQ+ rights, for example, can evolve over time as they learn more. (To be clear, sexual harassment, discrimination, and racism were never ethically acceptable.)

Consider the relationship between the job and the misbehavior. Most important, consider the other people for whom you are responsible (employees, children, an elderly parent). For example, I wouldn't put someone who has stolen money in charge of finances or hire someone with a DUI (driving under the influence citation) to be a driver.

There are some red lines. Candidates with a history of hate speech should not be put in situations of responsibility for vulnerable people, like caring for children, working in hospitals or assisted living facilities, or working with people with disabilities, addictions, or mental health issues.

If we reject someone who has made a past mistake, where does that leave us when we err ourselves? We could be missing an opportunity to make a difference in someone else's life—and our own. We each have the power to model and spread ethical behavior; giving others a second chance can be an opportunity to spread hope, compassion, and transparency. Not giving others (and ourselves) space to learn and change can also catalyze insidious drivers of unethical behavior—particularly perfectionism, shame, and the sense that there's no point in trying. That said, while a second chance might be the ethical path, a twenty-second chance is willful blindness.

Are we responsible for acting on information obtained without permission?

magine that you glanced at your colleague's computer screen while she steps away to refill her coffee or attend a meeting. The details aren't important except one: you didn't have permission to look. Now you have information that you wouldn't otherwise have. It appears as if your colleague is claiming some remote workdays that she took as vacation days recently. No one else would know, as she does a lot of independent work on projects remotely.

Or consider a variation of that scenario: you see a text on your spouse's or partner's phone without permission, a reminder for a Gamblers Anonymous (GA) meeting. An addiction can be very difficult for even those close to the person to detect. You had no idea, and you are very concerned, not least because your partner kept it from you. And you can't help but wonder—if your partner has been gambling, where has the money come from? How long has this been going on?

Exploration

This question hinges on whether how we *obtain* information affects the ethics of our decision.

Whether a discovery is accidental or intentional, remember, you may not know what you think you know. Perhaps your colleague's boss gave special permission for additional vacation days. Or maybe she misunderstood the policy and made an honest mistake. You don't know whether this is a first offense or an escalating pattern—or even if she followed through with the request. And your partner's Gamblers Anonymous meeting may have been an appointment to support a friend. (Whatever the situation is, seeking help, and helping others to seek help, is admirable and courageous.) Ethics start with questioning rather than accusing.

Next, consider the potential consequences of your decision, particularly those that are important and irreparable. What if you accidentally see an email in which a colleague asks an employee to delete an inspection report, or an email that contains harassment—behaviors that could result in real harm? Or some financial dishonesty that affects clients and the reputation of the company? Failure to report more serious situations could result in the person continuing the wrongdoing, harm to the company and others, and consequences for you if you have an obligation under company policies to report misconduct. Consider also the extent to which the issue is within your own realm of responsibility. And yes, reporting also risks rupturing your relationship with your colleague.

When ethical decisions go awry, we should ask what the perpetrator *knew*, *could have known*, or *should have known*. Unfortunately, the first perpetrator here is *you—you* obtained information without permission. The twist here is that you know, but should not have known.

The next challenge is whether and how to divulge the information you have. Ask the person directly involved; don't consult Human Resources, the person's manager, or another third party. Once you share information, you can't un-share it. If you're wrong, you don't want false ac- cusations floating around—or accurate reports that you're not minding your own business. You owe the other person privacy and the benefit of the doubt. Give the person a chance to fix the problem or come clean proactively. If they don't take action, then you can escalate your concern if the matter is serious enough.

What about your spouse or partner and Gamblers Anonymous? If you discover clues indicating that you are in a relationship with a compulsive gambler, speak directly to your partner. Addiction is a serious illness that scatters shrapnel far and wide, from co-addiction, to financial irresponsibility, to violating the law. It is a heartbreaking disease.

The bottom line is, if you come into the possession of important information, you have responsibility to prevent possible serious harm, however you obtained it. Make sure one ethical misstep doesn't beget another, such as by lying to cover up what you know. There's a fine line between "it's not your story to tell" and "it's a story you must tell even if doing so reveals the questionable way you learned of the story in the first place."

Would you apply for a job that your friend is also applying for?

I magine that you have been working hard in the marketing department of a company for several years, when you learn of an opening for an art director. These roles are rare, and it seems like a fantastic opportunity. But your best friend heard of it online, too, and confides in you excitedly that she is sending in her résumé. Do you still pursue it?

Exploration

Lebanese poet and author Kahlil Gibran wrote that "friendship is always a sweet responsibility, never an opportunity." Of the many conversations I had in researching this book, this one turned out to be one of the most difficult for many people because it challenges us to consider more broadly how we would behave as a friend.

Start with the principles at stake, because they establish who you are and how you want to behave toward others: respect, accountability, kindness, nonjudgment, and honesty.

These principles would most likely encourage you to tell your friend that you are applying for the job as soon as you make the decision—not after you have the third round of interviews. Whatever your friend's response, you will have given her a chance to discuss this with you before you proceed. You will have acted in a way that builds trust over time, even if it introduces strain.

Consider what and who else matters. Is this truly your dream job? Are you desperately in need of it to meet family obligations? Or are you in a rewarding role already and just interested in testing the waters? Answer the same questions for your friend. Then let her answer these questions. Friendships based on honesty and respect should be able to withstand this effort to grapple with the situation, over time. Does your friendship genuinely support you in seizing new opportunities and being your best self? Is there anything in your situation that would suggest that the risk to your friendship is not worth it? Would your evaluation of the situation change if your friend is recovering from a serious illness, or is a single parent with young children to care for?

Remember, you are not making the decision about who gets the job. The employer is. Most employers take a number of factors into account—skills and experience, diversity in hiring, passion, a candidate's commitment to the job, longer-term ambitions, and culture fit. Deciding not to apply may have no bearing over whether your friend gets the job.

We don't have an ethical responsibility to give up job

opportunities—or our dreams. Nor do we get a pass for not telling our friend, applying, and not getting the job. There's no risk-free option here.

Friends frequently try out for the same sports teams, audition for the same plays, pursue the same senior roles in a company. Trust is built on truth—not on winning or losing a job or a sporting event.

There are some hard lines—you don't try to nudge a friend out of applying for the job, or speak ill of your friend during the recruiting process, should that occasion arise. Now, consider this variation: you only learn about this dream job through your friend. Does that change your answer?

Sometimes the seemingly commonplace dilemmas are the most difficult of all.

What are the ethical considerations of blind hiring?

I n 1969, the New York Philharmonic was accused of racial discrimination by two Black musicians. The New York City Commission on Human Rights ruled against the musicians but concluded that aspects of the way the orchestra hired were discriminatory. At the time, American orchestras were made up primarily of white male musicians. In an attempt to avoid bias, a number of orchestras in the 1970s and 1980s began using blind auditions, whereby candidates perform behind a screen so that judges base their decisions of whom to hire on their ears rather than potentially prejudging a candidate based on their own biases regarding race or gender. While this hiring system has appeared to significantly increase the number of female musicians among American orchestras, a 2016 report by the League of American Orchestras stated that between 2002 and 2014, "the proportion of Hispanic/Latino musicians started at 1.8 percent . . . and grew to just 2.5 percent," and "the proportion of African American musicians hovered at around 1.8 percent."

Exploration

Most of us aren't auditioning musicians in our daily lives. But there is increasing pressure on employers across industries from start-ups to major financial services firms to hire diverse staff. Blind hiring practices remove key candidate information from the recruiting process, such as one's photo, name, and identity, in an effort to prevent bias on the basis of gender, race, age, religion, and background. New technology has facilitated early-stage filtering of candidate information.

Arguments against blind hiring include the fact that candidates' personal information can only be hidden during the initial stage; in the interview stage, various aspects of identity are revealed. Additionally, candidates lose the opportunity to explain any negatives on their résumé that might eliminate them early on, such as a candidate who temporarily left the workforce to care for children or an elderly parent. Blind hiring may dismantle affirmative action efforts where they exist. And the technology used to screen candidates can skew results. In 2015, Amazon discovered that the AI in the experimental hiring tool they used to evaluate candidates was biased against women, because the data it relied on came from a time when most résumés were from men.

Blind recruiting processes work best where technical skills are a priority. Where people skills are critical, employers or recruiters should be more flexible to fit the job with the skills needed.

When I chair search committees, I ask search firms to explain their own efforts to seek out diversity and inclusion, and to show me their data. I also always ask to see stretch candidates who may not seem like an obvious fit or quite ready for the role but who might be able to grow into the role.

In all cases, what comes next is just as important: the commitment on the part of the organization to assure integration into the position, mentoring opportunities, providing resources to facilitate a new hire's success, and oversight of compensation and career advancement. Being hired is just the first step in becoming a valued and successful employee, just as hiring is just the first step in employers' responsibility to assure a diverse and thriving work environment.

Should employers be permitted to consult candidates' social media accounts as part of the recruiting process?

You are applying for a job you really want, whether it's a dream career move or a temporary stint to help you supplement income. And you're wondering whether the employer will check your social media. After all, you found the job through a listing on a social media site. The job description and recruiting instructions didn't mention anything about it. You're wondering what you can reasonably expect, and how you might respond to inquiries about any questionable postings you might have if they do check your social media.

According to Pew Research Center, seven in ten adults are on Facebook, and seven out of ten of those users visit the site at least once a day. LinkedIn, the professional networking site, now has 800 million members, with 99 percent of the Fortune 500 having a presence on LinkedIn. Many employers today use social media, including Facebook, LinkedIn, Twitter, and Instagram, to post jobs and look up information on potential candidates. Even families use social media to vet babysitters and other household service providers.

Exploration

So far there is seemingly little that candidates can do about employers using social media research in recruiting. On the other hand, social media has facilitated employment opportunities globally through job postings, helping connect companies and candidates.

Given how many people use social media professionally and personally, it has become one of the ways that many people present themselves to the world, and in the process the lines between our personal and professional lives have blurred.

Companies currently look on social media since it can indicate whether candidates might be respectful, creative, curious, and helpful—as well as reveal potentially worrisome content.

So how should employers think about their use of social media in the recruiting process? What should candidates know?

Employers should have a clear job description on social media and in all postings for any positions they are looking to fill, listing the skills required, responsibilities, pay structure, hours, and any other unique considerations. Employers should be *transparent about whether they are consulting social media in making a hiring decision*. Hiring should involve a multipronged process, which, depending on the role, may include: résumé, statement of reasons for interest in the role, qualifications, interviews, references, and skills and personality tests. (In a family or other personal situation some of this may be less formal, but interviews and references are essential.) All of these steps underpin accountability for hiring for the right reasons, and putting any investigation into a candidate's social media in perspective.

Employers should give candidates an opportunity to explain anything troubling that appears on their social media—perhaps providing context or acknowledging a mistake. Employers will likely learn information on social media that could not be legally or ethically asked in an interview, so they should take extra care to handle properly any information that could trigger bias with regard to age, race, gender, sexual orientation, religious affiliation, marital status, children, and other protected characteristics. On the other hand, I wonder how employers can completely disregard ("un-know") information obtained without asking the candidate.

There are boundaries of privacy that companies should not cross, such as asking for candidates' passwords or raising questions about other individuals who appear in posts. Probing a candidate's understanding of what is and isn't appropriate to post on social media when in the role, however, is fair game.

As a candidate, when an employer does an internet search, your social media will appear. It is unrealistic to think that your public postings will not be seen (both past and future posts, once you are hired). Assume everything you post could end up in employers' hands. (I had one case where a former college roommate of a candidate sent a screenshot of a now twenty-eight-year-old's racist tweets from college to a new employer. He was immediately fired.) And be honest in the interview. Whatever you may have posted, or done, dishonesty will only further undermine the ethics and destroy trust.

Are you obligated to report colleagues having a relationship?

You become aware that a manager of another group in your company has started to date someone more junior in her department—perhaps one of them has told you they went out to dinner or went dancing together. You're not sure if you have an obligation to say anything to Human Resources, or to the manager's boss.

I have seen many examples like this in my work as an ethics advisor: The head of the London office of a company dating the head of a division. A junior manager who didn't know how to handle her (unverified) sense that two of her direct reports were in a budding relationship. A story that hit the media of a CEO dating an outside consultant hired by the company. But uncomfortable situations can arise in nonromantic situations, as well. In one such case two senior managers had been college dorm buddies. Each hired extensively from their college and continued to socialize as a pack; those who weren't graduates of the university felt increasingly excluded.

Exploration

This question hinges on conflicts of interest—situations in which people might act out of personal interest (protecting their relationships) rather than in line with their professional responsibilities and in the best interest of the organization. Conflicts of interest can spur the spreading of unethical behavior, including unfairness or impunity, to fear, secrets, gossip, and even sexual harassment or bullying.

The practical fallout is that office environments become uncomfortable, trust falters because everyone knows about the secret, stress levels skyrocket, and the potential for unfairness increases.

Companies should require employees involved in a relationship with other employees or external providers to disclose the relationship confidentially to Human Resources or a manager relatively early on. The trouble comes with determining what "early on" means. It's tricky. Not after a first date, certainly, but well before your relationship has become office gossip.

Work relationships should be off limits for anyone in a senior leadership role. There is such a power imbalance with senior leaders, and their reach is so broad, that there is no conflict-free space. The same is true for compliance, Human Resources, and legal teams, even at more junior levels, because they have access to, and responsibility over, confidential files and decisions. On the other hand, junior employees, particularly in different offices, divisions, or specialties and reporting lines (no common boss or dependency on each other's work such as colleagues on a team), should be able to have properly reported relationships. People meet romantic partners at work. I believe companies should set clear and reasonable boundaries and reporting requirements, and then stay out of employees' private lives.

By reporting confidentially to an Ombuds service or to Human Resources, you're (rightly) making the ethics question the company's responsibility to determine whether the relationship is appropriate, and how to manage it. I don't recommend speaking to the individuals involved directly, unless one of them has confided in you (in which case you can urge them to report the relationship themselves). It could damage your office relationships or position you as a meddler, and you may not have accurate information about the relationship, or whether or not it was already reported. The best option may be to stay silent if the situation has no impact on your own work.

If and when you do report a relationship, keep in mind that the company doesn't owe you an explanation for how and why they resolved the issue. Potential solutions may include moving one or both employees into different roles, or locations, or one participant leaving the organization. Companies should take extra care to ensure that women and the more junior employees are not unfairly penalized.

Personal behavior belongs outside the office, whether or not relationships are reported.

Do I need to take unconscious bias training every year?

In the late 1980s when I started out as a young lawyer, a friend who worked at an investment bank described something called diversity training as part of her introduction for new hires. She saw it as a good-faith initiative from well-intentioned leaders, but felt the questions were absurd (even by late 1980s standards). One hypothetical scenario probed what they should do if an important client inappropriately suggested a wet T-shirt contest at a deal-closing event. Another was blatantly homophobic. This training primarily targeted new recruits; she never received an invitation to a second round of training. It also seemed more focused on getting the "right answer" to various scenarios than actually training young bankers to recognize, and commit to eradicating, bias, discrimination, and inequality in real life.

The term "implicit bias" or "unconscious bias" refers to our "attitudes and beliefs that occur outside of our conscious awareness and control."

Exploration

I have learned from research, experts, and professional situations that all humans experience unconscious bias regardless of their level of education, socioeconomic situation, seniority within an organization, and other factors—and that it wreaks havoc on our ethics. Eradicating unconscious bias requires a sustained lifelong commitment to learning to make us aware—conscious—of our biases. As professors Max H. Bazerman of Harvard and his co-author Ann E. Tenbrunsel point out in their book *Blind Spots: Why We Fail to Do What's Right and What to Do About It*, we're not as ethical in our decision making as we like to think we are. Unconscious bias is one reason for that. Racism and other forms of bias are enmeshed in our systems and institutions. But we as individuals have a responsibility to do our part as well.

Why is *regular* training so important? Bias cannot be eradicated through a single event or training session. Regular training can bring us up to date on how unconscious bias evolves, as our society evolves—such as how social media and photo-enhancing apps turbocharge bias, discrimination, and narrow-mindedness. In other words, bias training is never done.

Regular training can also help stop the spread—the normalization—of bias and the slipping back into blind spots. But it's like a medical checkup: you need to have it done periodically. Regular training can also hold a mirror up to arrogance, the belief that we know enough, or that we're somehow special and exempt from this all-too-human foible.

Unconscious bias training can be particularly helpful in hiring decisions, including by reinforcing good listening skills and questioning our own perspectives. It is a way of pressing pause—reminding us that bias can cause us to leap to uninformed decisions and helping us to *see people for who they are* instead of the broad brushstrokes that fit them neatly into easily identifiable buckets such as race, creed, sexual orientation, or political party affiliation.

Some people claim that training isn't helpful or enough. I don't comment here on the specifics of any particular approach to training. Quality varies. And no one strategy suffices; training is one of many tools we should incorporate to increase our awareness of unconscious bias and change our behavior. In fact, one of the biggest mistakes organizations make is assuming unconscious bias training is the solution instead of part of the fight against bias.

But I have seen firsthand that by making the unconscious conscious, on an ongoing basis, we are better able to gain perspective on our ethics—better able to see our decisions while walking in someone else's shoes.

We're only as ethical as our last decisions. Regularly updated unconscious bias training can help us see some of our most important ethical weaknesses, decision by decision.

Chapter 4

Technology

Should social media companies shut down accounts of the president of the United States and other political leaders if they incite violence?

n a post dated January 7, 2021—the day after the insurrection of the U.S. Capitol—Facebook CEO Mark Zuckerberg put an indefinite suspension on President Donald Trump's Facebook and Instagram accounts, claiming he was using "our platform to incite violent insurrection . . . We believe the risks of allowing the President to continue to use our service during this period are simply too great." A day later, Twitter CEO Jack Dorsey suspended Donald Trump's Twitter account, @realDonaldTrump, permanently. In June 2021, Facebook announced Trump would be banned until at least January 2023, when the company would reevaluate his eligibility.

The Supreme Court has only recently begun to confront the impact of the internet and social media on First Amendment issues. One example: in its unanimous 2017 opinion in *Packingham v. North Carolina*, the Court invalidated a North Carolina statute that made it a felony for a registered sex offender to log on to a commercial social networking site known to be accessible to minors. Even then, the Court recognized how quickly obsolete its rulings involving technology and the internet may be, with its "vast potential to alter how we think, express ourselves, and define who we want to be."

Exploration

Free speech is critical to ethics and democracy. Without it, truth, a nonnegotiable foundation for ethical decisions, collapses. Free speech can come under threat through government censorship, algorithms that spread disinformation, face-to-face, or online.

While the First Amendment to the Constitution prohibits the federal government from "abridging the freedom of speech, or of the press; or the right of the people peaceably to assemble," it doesn't prohibit corporations or private businesses like Twitter and Facebook from regulating speech, or establishing rules or terms of service. And they remain responsible for protecting and promoting free speech—and for setting boundaries to prevent real harm—as a matter of ethics. (Twitter and Facebook may not technically be media companies, but they function as such when they become both the access point for media and an influence on the media we see through their algorithms.)

Whenever considering a politically sensitive ethics

question, I suggest hypothetically replacing the political party in question with the party you support. Can you in good faith still dismantle the other side's arguments?

Second, safety and rule of law should prevail. We may need to shift our views of what words we consider "inciting violence" in a world in which social media instantaneously shares our messages to millions.

Who gets to decide? We don't want the CEOs of Amazon, Apple, Google, Facebook, TikTok, and Twitter arbitrating our societal conversations (and for the most part they don't want to), or becoming the determiners of truth. (Although they may do so indirectly as they did when Apple and Google removed Parler, the alternative social media app favored by conservatives, from their app stores for failing to remove dangerous content, and Amazon suspended Parler from its web hosting service.) And we rightly adhere to the First Amendment to prevent government censorship. But each of us individually also has a responsibility as we use these platforms, for the information we choose to post, read, and reshare. Without us, those inciting violence don't have an audience.

Ethical decisions require considering the actual and potential consequences: not what we know will happen, but what *could* happen. We had countless examples of unacceptable rhetoric and behavior on January 6—from politicians and ordinary citizens (including calls for combat and threats of revenge for failure to join the insurrection). It shouldn't take five people dying at the riot and more dying afterward to take action.

We must distinguish among various types of speech and determine which are to be protected (even if offensive) and which are to be prohibited, such as hate speech inciting violence, bullying, and harassment.

I believe in diverse voices, vigorous debate, and tolerating even offensive speech. But freedom of speech cannot mean freedom to harm.

Would you use the free Spotify service if you knew that artists are penalized financially?

In 2014, Taylor Swift pulled her discography from Spotify to protest what she saw as Spotify's unfair treatment of artists. Her battle highlighted the fact that Spotify offers consumers a choice between free music with advertising or paid subscriptions with no ads. "It's my opinion," Swift argued in a *Wall Street Journal* op-ed, "that music should not be free." She then released her album *1989* that same year, avoiding streaming platforms. Swift later returned to the platform in 2017 after a new licensing deal between her distributor Universal Music Group and Spotify allowed artists to withhold new releases from free subscribers for a period of time so the artists could potentially make more money.

With music streaming, you can listen to music without downloading song files to your computer hard drive. Spotify compensates the rights holders of music (e.g., record labels, distributors, aggregators, collection societies) through a concept called "streamshare": payment is based on the proportion of the streams of an artist's music (relative to the total number of streams) in a given month in a given market. Artists are then compensated by the rights holders, as spelled out in the terms of the artists' and labels' agreements. For example, Spotify says on its Loud & Clear microsite, if an artist (assuming they are the rights holder) received one in every 1,000 streams in Mexico in a given month, they would receive $1 of every $1,000 paid to rights holders from the royalty pool for the country. That includes subscription and music advertising revenue.

Spotify is the largest music-streaming service in the world in terms of the number of subscribers. In its 2021 third-quarter financial statement, Spotify reported that it had 172 million premium subscribers and 220 million ad-supported "monthly active users."

And independent and new, emerging artists may make very little in royalties. To give a sense of perspective, in 2020, the top 1 percent of artists accounted for 90 percent of all streams.

Exploration

On the positive side, Spotify provides access to a wide variety of music, encouraging a willingness to try new genres and artists given that we don't pay for each song we listen to. They offer lesser known artists access to a growing global audience. They spread culture, diversity, and even spirituality and joy. And they are sustainable: there is no packaging and no consumption of fossil fuels for transport. In addition, the advertising model makes music available for free to those who cannot afford the monthly premium subscription service or do not wish to pay.

By mid-2021, streaming accounted for 84 percent of recorded music revenue according to the Recording Industry Association of America. And it has increased recorded music revenue for musicians. As Princeton economics professor Alan B. Krueger noted in his book *Rockonomics*, from 2015 to 2017 revenue from recorded music—primarily as a result of streaming—increased by $2 billion, "erasing the last ten years of declines and providing a much-needed boost to the music industry." Paid subscription streaming services have continued to experience double-digit retail growth in the U.S., reaching 75.5 million in 2020 according to the RIAA.

On the other hand, Spotify, along with Apple Music, Google Play Music, Amazon Music, YouTube Music, and others, is also part of a trend in platform monopolization laden with ethics risks. Its technology disintermediates, or removes the middle players, such as retail stores. For many of us, our relationships with musicians now exist through a tech platform on which the royalty system can distort results. Users who spend more time on the platform and stream more often have a greater influence on which artists are paid more (even though users all pay the same subscription fee). These platforms feed arbitrariness (a driver of unethical behavior) by unlinking our purchasing choices from the financial reward—in this case, for artists and their art.

My view is that ethics should not, and need not, impede

this important innovation giving millions of people access to music and artists access to a vast listening public. It's a technological version of museums opening their doors for free to some patrons or putting virtual exhibits online free of charge. But the ethical responsibility is shared. Spotify must protect artists' intellectual property and monitor the fairness of the streaming business model, particularly for artists with smaller audience bases. As consumers we must recognize that opting for free by putting up with the occasional ad affects artists as well (unlike with our free use of social media in exchange for targeted ads). And artists should consider the economic and artistic benefits of a larger fan base and their responsibility to the public.

Should social media companies be required to offer users the option to pay a fee to avoid receiving targeted advertising?

I ordered a pair of flip-flops through a website, and now the company's advertisements pop up on my screen constantly. It's annoying. I don't need more footwear or other unsolicited recommendations. On the other hand, a friend's son was looking for an app to implement a tutoring service he and friends were setting up. Two weeks after an unsuccessful search, he was thrilled to receive an unsolicited targeted ad with just the product they needed.

Online advertising targets individuals based on data collected about each individual user, such as from their Facebook profile. Marketers can pinpoint ads to us based on what we like and what we buy. Depending on your sensitivity, targeting can seem invasive or even creepy. It assesses such characteristics as age, gender, income, attitudes, activity, location, and internet searches over time to predict your preferences.

Exploration

This is not a life-and-death situation. But it is one with consequences that will ripple throughout society, particularly as technology behemoths collect more and more data from us, and exercise the ability to control and use that data.

Targeted ads affect every one of us who has an online presence. They also raise broader societal questions about who should benefit from, and control, our personal data. In 2019, Facebook had ad revenue of $69.7 billion; more than 98 percent of the company's global revenue came from advertising. Facebook's share of the U.S. digital advertising market in 2020 was 25.2 percent, while Google's was even higher, at 28.9 percent.

Consider the positives: some consumers like seeing opportunities and find ads efficient; ad revenue makes Google Search and Calendar or Facebook and Messenger available free to billions of people around the world; small businesses are able to reach distant, otherwise inaccessible audiences; and sometimes lifesaving information pops up at just the right time—such as about the rising Covid-19 infections in your area during the pandemic.

A significant objection to a payment option is that it results in inequality: users who can't afford to pay would have no choice but continue to give up their data, and receive targeted ads, in exchange for the free service. Unlike other premium services like Amazon Prime or Apple TV+, social media can touch on our livelihood, family, and news sources.

And the data set could be skewed toward people who can't pay, which in turn might embed in the data additional inequality linked to race, gender, and access to technology; such skewed and distorted data could be dangerous in systems linked to health, voting, and other civic matters.

With or without payment, many stakeholders share responsibility for targeted advertising. Governments should regulate social media companies more carefully, particularly for issues such as truth in advertising, risk of fraud, and age appropriateness. And why couldn't social media companies make free services available to those who couldn't pay while diminishing the number of ads they are subjected to?

As much as search and social media companies have democratized access to these platforms, a fundamental question remains. Should the data these companies collect be allowed to be monopolized and controlled as private property (for shareholder benefit), or should the data be required to be made public (for public benefit such as mental health and education research)?

I often hear in conversations among experts that "people are just willing to live with the consequences" in exchange for free access to services. I'm not convinced of our willingness, or even our freedom of choice, when no one I know (including myself) is able to fully understand the terms of service of social media companies or articulate accurately the long-term ethical consequences of free social media.

Would you agree to let your elderly loved one be cared for by a robot?

Meet Zora. Just under five feet tall, "she" is a humanoid robot with sensors that allow her to "see" and "hear." She can tell stories, teach programming to her human companions, and play games. She is programmable through a touch panel and is easily transportable. She shrugs her shoulders, dances, demonstrates gym moves as an exercise class leader—thanks to joints in her legs, arms, and digits. She has a built-in camera that allows her to scan barcodes. And she can interact with people of all age groups, from offering homework assistance for kids, to acting as a personal trainer for fitness-focused adults, to serving as a companion for older adults in elder care facilities. She was specifically designed to meet human social needs and "accompany you throughout your day with a positive attitude."

Zora is not alone. PARO is a therapeutic companion robot in the form of a stuffed seal that is found to ease patient stress and improve socialization. In early 2020, as

I entered the European office of a client I was advising, a humanoid robot, known as Pepper, greeted me. I had a touch screen exchange with Pepper, to which Pepper responded by flashing the organization's ethical principles.

South Korea stepped up its use of robots during Covid-19 with robots that spray disinfecting agents, check temperatures, and detect mask wearing (while protecting privacy by blurring faces).

Exploration

When discussing robots, it is important to start with humancentric ethics concerns, such as health and safety, respect, privacy, and compassion.

Robots are tools—no more human than washing machines. They are intended to supplement human care—a friend or a relative visiting, or other human contact—not replace it. We should prioritize human beings in making decisions about whether to use or deploy a robot. The goal is to maximize benefits to patients (reducing loneliness, increasing engagement, and augmenting care, such as checking blood pressure and providing medications) and mitigate risks (privacy violations or insufficient human oversight). The population of adults over the age of sixty-five is expected to more than double to more than 1.5 billion by 2050, according to the United Nations, making supplemental care increasingly important.

It's easy to assume that patients prefer interactions with other human beings. But nonhuman assistance might offer the person being cared for greater privacy and independence—such as in assisting with personal hygiene. Some caregivers have reported that the elderly share emotions more freely with robots that they wouldn't share with staff. Robots may also reduce the workload for caregivers, allowing staff more time to devote to more critical medical and psychological concerns.

As with any medical intervention, informed consent is vital. Not all elderly people have the capacity to grant consent, as in the case of dementia. Families need to be informed by hospitals and care centers before robot care is incorporated, and grant specific consent.

For perspective, we can look at this question on a spectrum of other options, from full-time human care, an option that may not be possible for many of us, to no human care. In between, there might be a mix of human care and robot care, with the engagement of the medical professionals in charge. Such care could include video check-ins or full medical sessions with caregivers, data gathered for caregivers via internet-connected devices, and online cognitive training.

Finally, how do we allocate responsibility for any harm (including misuse of data) to a person caused by a robot? Is the medical facility responsible? The individual caregiver deploying the robot? The manufacturer? For me, the physician or other human overseer must be held accountable—just as they would for a recommendation of any other treatment or use of a medical device. But we should be able to rely on proper transparency and safeguards from companies, as well, and regulators should sign off on robots' use for medical interventions.

As David Hanson, founder of Hanson Robotics and creator of the humanoid robot Sophia, told me, robots may call on us to be better human beings—perhaps even better caregivers, friends, and family members.

Should police departments be allowed to use facial recognition technology?

O n a Thursday afternoon in 2020, Robert Julian-Borchak Williams, who worked in an automotive supply company, was arrested in his driveway by two police officers as his family looked on. Matched by a facial recognition algorithm to blurred video surveillance tape, Williams, who is Black, was charged with shoplifting at an upscale boutique in October 2018. But the algorithm was wrong: Williams was innocent.

Facial recognition technology, or FRT, uses computer algorithms to analyze details about a person's face, and compare that information against photographs in a database of known individuals.

Driven to a detention center, Williams was booked, fingerprinted, and held for over thirty hours. This became the first known case of an American mistakenly arrested due to faulty facial recognition software.

FRT can be used in two ways: for *verification*, where an image of a person is scanned and compared to a known image in a database, such as a passport photo; and for *identification*, where police take an unknown face off surveillance images and look for a match.

Verification, according to the National Institute of Standards and Technology (NIST), is highly accurate. With good-quality photos, the most accurate algorithms have miss rates of less than 1 percent. But identification, as in the case of Robert Williams, is far less accurate; it is much harder for a fixed camera to take high-quality photos of people on the move, obscured by shadows and other people.

Exploration

If we're trying to find a terrorist or a lost child, we would be in favor of facial recognition technology. If we're trying to eliminate racial and other types of profiling, and protect the privacy of innocent citizens, we would be vehemently against it. The paramount concerns to consider here are safety, privacy, respect, antidiscrimination, transparency, and legal compliance.

Many police departments, as well as the Department of Homeland Security, are embracing these FRT tools, saying they can help them more efficiently identify and arrest criminals. But FRT can result in misidentification, false positives, racial bias, and the apprehension of innocent citizens. In 2018, the American Civil Liberties Union reported that Amazon's FRT incorrectly matched twenty-eight members of Congress with people who had been arrested. A 2018 study of gender and skin-color bias in three commercial AI systems found an error rate that was never greater than 0.8 percent in light-skinned men, but which "ballooned" to as much as 46.8 percent for dark-skinned women.

In 2020, Massachusetts became the first state to join cities like Portland, Maine, and Portland, Oregon, as well as San Francisco and Oakland, to ban police use of facial recognition technology. In 2020, Microsoft announced that the company won't sell facial recognition technology to police departments until there is a "national law in place grounded in human rights." Amazon initially followed suit with a one-year moratorium, which they extended in 2021 until further notice.

The caution exhibited by Microsoft and Amazon has been emulated by Clearview AI, a start-up company that has "shrouded itself in secrecy," creating and selling a game-changing facial recognition app that has a database of 3 billion images that the company has taken from Facebook, YouTube, and the like. The *New York Times* reports that more than six hundred law enforcement agencies and a handful of companies have already started using it to identify people and potentially review their social contacts and where they live and work. But there has been pushback. Facebook announced the imminent closure worldwide of its facial recognition system. And in 2021 Clearview was banned from scraping images from websites in Australia; its services are already banned in Canada.

Lawmakers, corporations, police forces, and regulators

at least owe the public transparency about what FRT does, and how human checks and balances can be incorporated.

The bottom line is that we need to monitor progress in the technology; engage the public, corporations, and government in the debate; and press pause until we can eliminate bias and establish ethical and legal guardrails—while looking for ways to carve out exceptions in extreme cases such as a lost child or an active terrorist threat.

How do we handle the ethics of a deceased loved one's social media accounts?

One of my students told the class about her pursuit of the truth behind the kind of person her mother was by reading her late mother's diary. She discovered that her experience of growing up with her mother was skewed by the fact that she only partially understood her mother's past. Her lifelong condemnation of her mother's selfishness and indifference gave way to admiration for the quiet sacrifice her mother made to raise a family in the U.S., far from her country of birth. She learned how her mother navigated a multiracial marriage and parenting challenges. The diary shed light on her own multiracial identity growing up, her childhood family experiences, and her ability to rise to the highest echelons of business.

Her discovery of the truth about her mother and her family hinged on a single document—the diary, a physical object that only she could read and which she kept in her possession. Neither she nor her mother had posted it or made entries on social media. The daughter controlled whether or not to share it with others, and the decision of how much of it she might share. And who would inherit the diary after her own death.

She wondered what she would do if, like her own journal, the diary had been in the form of a Facebook, Instagram, or other social media accounts.

Exploration

Sharing a deceased person's private social media account is an ethical minefield. We cannot know what was happening in their heart or mind when they posted content, or how their views might have changed over time. We lack context. We don't know if an image was photoshopped, or our relative was having a bad day. We don't know how much of our loved one's account they would wish to share with us, let alone allow us to share with others.

Losing this content, however, might destroy the person's personal history with, and connection to, other relatives, not to mention erase an opportunity to honor a loved one's life.

There is a quagmire of ethics challenges for society, as well. Are social media accounts property, to be disposed of in a will just as a bank account or favorite necklace? Or is it a contract between you and the social media company to be disposed of according to their terms of service? State laws regarding posthumous privacy are evolving.

The diary of my student's mother was just as much a part of her belongings and inheritance as any family heirloom she received. Her mother likely could not have imagined that her diary would be shared with others beyond her immediate family, let alone potentially with strangers who with the click of a button could reshare. On the other hand, while her daughter had to consider her mother's privacy, I think her daughter's choice (to read it in confidence and then decide how to handle it) was the only option that didn't have important and irreparable consequences (destroying a family heirloom without knowing what's in it).

I am staunchly committed to truth and to avoiding "all or nothing" situations. I would be inclined to preserve the diary and pass it on to a very limited group of people who agreed to keep it confidential and respect the conditions of the deceased's will. I might share specific sections with individuals for whom it might bring joy or reassurance. I would never post, or repost, any of the diary on social media or in electronic form because technology dramatically increases the dissemination of material in ways that I cannot control.

We should also ask whether it's our story to tell. If our relative had wanted to share more widely, I assume they would have. And we are not the only stakeholder in our decision. The information that other people shared with the deceased was also private and not intended to be shared more broadly without permission.

Society's ethical norms have not caught up with the increasingly frequent decision of whether and when to expose social media without permission. Social media companies' terms of use should tell us in plain language what happens to our data upon our death. (Deletion? Appointing a guardian? Preserved as a memorial?)

If you are concerned about your own accounts, declare your wishes for posthumous social media, including in your will if you have one. Go to the sites and make choices about such things as legacy accounts and memorializing—and communicate your wishes to loved ones.

Would you consider using a bot therapist or recommending one for a family member or friend?

The daughter of someone I know has been diagnosed with depression. But their financial resources available to pay for individual therapy, which can cost $200 or more a session, several times a week, are limited.

One option the family considered is AI-powered Woebot, the "friendly little bot who's ready to listen 24/7." Woebot's mission, according to Woebot Health, is expanding access to mental health care. Woebot "works by inviting people to have a conversation," available any time of day or night "at a moment's notice." Woebot guides users to identify patterns in their moods and claims a 98.9 percent "accuracy rate in detecting crisis language"—but acknowledges that there is "no replacement for human connection." There are adolescent, maternal mental health, and substance use specialty options. Replika is a bot companion app (that doesn't claim to do therapy), allowing users to talk about their "thoughts, feelings, beliefs, experiences, memories, dreams" to a computer-generated digital companion, without humans in the loop. The app has been downloaded more than 2 million times. Other apps specialize, such as Pear Therapeutics' FDA-approved cognitive therapy apps for substance use disorders.

Mental health challenges are a global epidemic. The World Health Organization (WHO) reports that more than 700,000 people die around the world due to suicide every year. It is the fourth leading cause of death in people aged fifteen to nineteen worldwide. Nearly two thirds of those with a mental disorder "never seek help from a health professional," according to WHO.

Exploration

There are robust medical and professional ethics codes and oversight processes for human mental health professionals. This question targets what is ethically different about bot therapists, compared to human therapists.

The first challenge here is the huge gap in the information we need—we simply do not yet have sufficient data on the efficacy and risks of bot therapists trained on mountains of data versus a therapist's graduate degree and experience. This means that we cannot assess the immediate and longer-term consequences for patients, their families, and others affected. And without adequate information, our informed consent is not really informed.

What bot therapists potentially offer patients includes:

broad access to help for people who would otherwise be unable to afford a therapist, especially over an extended period of time; help for patients who are uncomfortable talking with another person about their struggles; and a complement to professional therapists. Some people may open up more knowing that they are talking to a bot. Risks of bot therapy include: data privacy breaches; therapeutic risk (what happens if a bot can't recognize an individual's suicidal tendencies, can't prescribe medication, or can't otherwise help the patient?); exacerbating medical care inequality by replacing trained therapists with a bot in underserved areas; and, again, a dearth of research on therapeutic efficacy and harm.

One crucial factor here is determining who is responsible for any potential harm to the user—the company that builds, programs, and sells the bot? Its shareholders? Regulators who allow its use? The patient? On the other hand, human therapists, too, have varying degrees of ethical and legal responsibility to patients when harm occurs.

My own view is that AI for health care requires human supervision—but without compromising confidentiality. Like all technology that affects health and data privacy, regulators should set rigorous standards for the technology, transparency about the risks, and medical intervention.

Bot therapists are one of many innovations blurring the boundaries of humanity—assuming a role in one of the most fundamentally human areas of our lives, involving our emotions, well-being, brain chemistry, and relationships with medical professionals. Our ethics (and ultimately our laws) must restore those boundaries of human responsibility and assure transparency and truly informed consent to users and the public—without sacrificing much-needed access to care.

Do you have an obligation
to inform guests that you
have a digital assistant on in
your home when they visit?

One night, I was visiting a friend and as she was making dinner she turned to her Amazon Echo, and asked, "Alexa, what's the weather going to be in London tomorrow?" The device came to life at the sound of "Alexa," and gave her a forecast of rain. I was uncomfortable with the idea of Alexa "listening" to me. The device stayed quiet through dinner, and I forgot about it for the most part. But on my way home I couldn't help wondering if it was off, or listening, or perhaps listening and recording. I knew the Alexa personal assistant is only supposed to activate with key wake words. But there have been plenty of news reports of conversations accidentally recorded. Who knows if parts of our conversation had been recorded by Alexa and sent to the cloud and, if so, whether Amazon employees or others could access it?

Today in the U.S., one in four of us keep, on average, 2.6 smart speaker devices in our homes. At CES 2020, the largest technology convention in the world (originally known as the Consumer Electronics Show), Amazon announced there were now "hundreds of millions of Alexa-enabled devices" in the hands of customers around the world—more than double from a year earlier.

Exploration

Every day, people around the world "wake up" their speakers and ask their digital voice assistants to play music, check their calendars, call up recipes or instructions, or check the weather. Alexa has become so convenient that for many it has become a part of their everyday lives, an adopted habit, the incredibly efficient and reliable personal assistant you never had. But not everyone is comfortable with them. At their core, Alexa, Siri and Google Assistant are data-gathering machines that record our conversations, unless we turn off the microphone.

The widespread use of Alexa and similar devices is a clue about a potential ethics pitfall: the more something becomes normal, the less we question its use and the more its use spreads. And this is even more true when the habit involves a technology device with rapidly changing capabilities.

The people affected by our use of Alexa include you and any guests to your home, their families, anyone they may have spoken about while at your house, as well as Amazon or the device's company and partners. They could include other companies Amazon may acquire in the future, Amazon employees, and contractors. And *how* they are affected could change in ways you would never know. As Amazon notes in their terms of service, "Amazon processes and retains your Alexa interactions, such as your voice inputs, music playlists, and your Alexa to-do and shopping lists, in the cloud." Moreover, they state that you "and all other persons who use Alexa under your account" agree to their terms of service by using Alexa. It is difficult for the average user to understand what information the company records, or how the company uses that data. Given that police have obtained court-ordered warrants for recordings, others affected can potentially even include law enforcement and the courts.

To me, truth, privacy, transparency, and respect are at stake—all essential to trusted friendship. Friends and guests to your home can reasonably expect that their conversations are private. Leaving a device on when friends are in your house, and unintentionally exposing their conversations to being recorded, can be seen as a serious breach of their trust. Moreover, if your guests are not aware that Alexa is on, they are not making choices for themselves. (Informed consent refers to choices we make based on a full understanding of the risks and benefits.)

That said, we shouldn't miss the opportunities Alexa offers, whether convenience or, more importantly, for people with a wide range of emotional and physical challenges, from mobility to communication.

The solution here is simple: turn off Alexa when friends come over, or inform your friends that it's on so that they can make the choice for themselves.

Would you use the Robinhood trading app?

On Monday, January 25, 2021, individual investors snatched up shares in struggling retail game company GameStop (GME) in droves through retail brokers and the commission-free trading app Robinhood. Some traders on WallStreetBets (a message board in the social media and community network platform Reddit) banded together to inflict losses on institutional investors engaged in short selling.

Robinhood's stated mission is to democratize trading—to befriend the small investor. One investment expert likened the GameStop buying frenzy to purchasing a lottery ticket. The stock price skyrocketed from $20 on Monday, January 11 to a high of almost $500 on Thursday, January 28. Much of the GameStop bubble was disconnected from the company's fundamentals—their revenues, operating expenses, profits, and potential for growth.

At the height of the unprecedented rally in the stock price of GameStop and other companies, more than 24 billion shares were traded on U.S. exchanges, a level that was more than six times the previous single-day record on Wall Street. The rally was the result of a so-called short squeeze. In a short squeeze, investor buying causes a rise in the stock price, forcing sellers who have shorted the stock—in expectation that the price would fall—to cover their position to avoid further losses. It revealed the power individual investors could wield on financial markets if enough of them bought a stock to cause an artificial spike in the share price.

But the mania backfired on the Robinhood site. As a result of the trading volatility, Robinhood's Wall Street clearinghouse increased their cash deposit requirements tenfold, to ensure that their trades were settled smoothly. (Clearinghouses are responsible for settling accounts and clearing trades, among other things.) As a result, on Thursday, January 28, Robinhood had to limit trading. Investors could no longer buy the stock—they could only sell what they had. Investors, the media, and Washington cried foul, and Robinhood customers expressed their anger on social media.

Exploration

Robinhood is an example of scattered power, one of the most influential forces driving how we make decisions. Sometimes scattered power involves many individual acts organized into a movement, such as a storm of small stock market trades.

Companies that provide the technology are the scatterers of the power. Robinhood benefits from scattering power because the more customers trade on Robinhood, the more money the company makes despite not charging commissions. Robinhood earns revenue from third parties that pay the company for the right to fulfill its trades (so-called payment for order flow). So Robinhood shares responsibility for misuse of the product and reasonably warning users of serious risk.

Robinhood should have known the major risks that could affect their customers: cash requirements for clearing, individual users potentially suffering significant financial loss or even becoming addicted to trading as a form of online gambling, and manipulative speculation. There is a robust history of securities law focused on protecting unsophisticated investors. The tech landscape is littered with companies that moved too quickly and harmed individuals.

With Robinhood, I do not believe investors understand what they are signing on for. There is no real informed consent. Robinhood's customer agreement at the time was thirty-three pages of legalese in eye-straining print. I understood very little of it (including the company's responsibility to me), despite my years as a securities lawyer at a top Wall Street firm and decades of ethics advisory work. Most users are inexperienced traders who don't fully understand the underlying financial risks. And Robinhood's business model is spreading; today many companies offer commission-free trading. In 2021, the company announced plans to undertake a coffeehouse tour of colleges to attract students and younger investors.

A lofty mission is only ethical when deployed ethically. Taking actions based on principles such as customer well-being and transparency is a start. Companies must ensure that customers fully understand the risks and are equipped to make their own ethical choices. Robinhood is also responsible for assuring sufficient liquidity to settle trades.

While as a general matter users of technology also have responsibility with respect to how they deploy their power and inform themselves of risks (or a company's failure to adequately explain risks), we cannot blame users for Robinhood's management of their brokerage. Hedge funds are experts in financial risk; they can quickly determine how to recoup the significant losses they incurred shorting GameStop shares. But Robinhood's weaknesses ultimately harm all investors and the public by undermining trust in financial markets. Finally, regulators, too, should have addressed the potential for this kind of trading risk with Robinhood's business model and adopted rules to limit the damage, especially to inexperienced investors. The fact that trading happens through an app, or free of commissions, doesn't change the fundamental ethics risk and responsibility. Ultimately, individual traders and their families were harmed.

Should Apple be required to unlock encrypted iPhones at the request of the FBI in an investigation of a terrorist act?

In December 2015, Syed Rizwan Farook, a county environmental inspector, and his wife, Tashfeen Malik, dressed in combat gear and wearing masks, entered the Inland Regional Center in San Bernardino, a nonprofit corporation that provides services and programs for people with disabilities, and opened fire with .223 caliber assault rifles. Firing over one hundred rounds within several minutes, they killed fourteen people and wounded twenty-two others before fleeing the scene. The two terrorists were killed in a shootout with police a few miles away.

The FBI, investigating the potential that others were involved in the San Bernardino attack, appealed to Apple to unlock Farook's encrypted iPhone. Apple and the Justice Department had been sparring with each other since the debut of the encrypted iOS 8 operating system in 2014. Apple said that the Justice Department was pushing them to create a backdoor—software code that would allow law enforcement to circumvent the password and unlock the encrypted devices. Apple resisted, offering alternative ways to obtain data from the phone. They explained that they didn't have a way to unlock the phone, without putting a team of software engineers on it to rewrite the operating system, which they refused to do.

In February, a federal district court judge issued a request to Apple to help unlock the phone. Apple appealed the request. CEO Tim Cook issued a letter to Apple customers, explaining the company's position: "We fear that this demand would undermine the very freedoms and liberty our government is meant to protect."

Ultimately, a third party—a little-known Australian cybersecurity firm called Azimuth Security—was able to unlock the phone, and the FBI withdrew its request to the court. But because the issue never went to trial, the long-running dispute between law enforcement and tech companies over privacy safeguards remains unresolved. (Apple is now suing Azimuth for their actions.) In fact, the situation recurred in December 2019 when the FBI asked Apple to help unlock two iPhones that belonged to the gunman who killed three sailors at Naval Air Station Pensacola. On its website, Apple claims that law enforcement departments have logged hundreds of requests with the company to unlock Apple phones.

Exploration

This case pits two critical principles against each other: safety and privacy. The FBI, investigating potential remaining threats from others who might have been involved in the San Bernardino shootings, was focused on ensuring the safety of American citizens.

Apple came down on the side of consumer privacy. But the company was also considering longer-term safety risks. As Tim Cook wrote, "Compromising the security of our personal information can ultimately put our personal safety at risk . . . Once created, the technique could be used over and over again." Apple also feared that foreign agents or authoritarian regimes could gain access to devices and put people at risk.

Privacy and consumer advocates supported Apple's position and Cook's response. Alex Abdo, then a staff lawyer for the American Civil Liberties Union, said, "Apple deserves praise for standing up for its right to offer secure devices." But law enforcement agencies criticized Apple just as strongly. Remember that the owner of the phone was a known terrorist (not a potential suspect), and he was dead (with potentially lesser privacy interests).

A few questions can help us test our views. How would the decision feel looking back on it from a future time? I asked a group of CEOs just after this incident how they would assess Cook's decision, or the opposite, weeks, months, even years out if a second related terrorist attack took place. And what would their decision look like from the perspective of different stakeholders—from other phone owners to law enforcement to potential victims of terrorist attacks?

Ethics, done well, should involve looking for alternatives. Apple did provide the data that they had on their servers, and suggested ways that the FBI could access some of the information on the phone. But they refused to help unlock the phone. The ultimate solution was an alternative actor (the Australian firm Azimuth).

Apple's promise to consumers, as they wrote on their website, was that "Apple cannot bypass your passcode and therefore cannot access this data." And so far, they have refused to create software that would give law enforcement a backdoor to unlock their phones. The commitment to keep their word to consumers is admirable. However, consumers deserve to know that while Apple might keep its promise not to bypass codes, other actors can.

Should robots have rights?

Sophia, the world's first humanoid robot, was invented by Hanson Robotics, and made "her" appearance before the public at the annual South by Southwest festival in Austin in 2016. The Hanson Robotics website describes Sophia as a humanlike robot that features "cutting edge robotics and AI research." Her face, made from patented elastic-rubber material, is strikingly human, modeled after ancient Egyptian queen Nefertiti and Hanson's wife in order to represent diverse physiques. She "can estimate your feelings during a conversation" and "has her own emotions too." She has appeared on *60 Minutes*, *The Tonight Show with Jimmy Fallon*, and *Good Morning Britain.*

Sophia's artificial intelligence enables her to "recognize human faces, see emotional expressions, and recognize various hand gestures." Sophia continually learns from the world around her through machine learning—the field within artificial intelligence "that gives computers the ability to learn without explicitly being programmed."

In 2017, Sophia became the first robot to be granted citizenship, by Saudi Arabia. The same year, the European Parliament adopted the resolution on Civil Law Rules on Robotics, which included a proposal to explore the creation of a special "legal status" for robots, allowing them to be "insured individually and held liable for damages if they go rogue." A backlash ensued, as over 156 experts from fourteen countries, in an open letter to the EU, expressed alarm, stating, "From an ethical and legal perspective, creating a legal personality for a robot is inappropriate."

Exploration

As robots and other versions of artificial intelligence increasingly infiltrate our lives, from flipping burgers to offering us viewing options based on our preferences on Netflix, the issue of whether robots should have rights is already squarely before society.

Robots may blur boundaries between human and machine, but in my view *human* rights must always take precedence. The question of robot rights is really a question of *human responsibility*.

We don't change our ethics foundations, such as safety, honesty, dignity, transparency, and compassion, just because robots are involved. People design, build, manufacture, program, and deploy robots; they must assure us that the robots they create act in furtherance of protecting and aiding us and preventing harm to humans. We shouldn't build driverless cars that preserve the car over saving the lives of passengers or pedestrians. We need to be assured that robots are ready to be trusted not to undercook a burger, mislabel a package, or spread hate speech on social media.

Whatever your view on robot rights, our behavior toward robots is important. We need more research on the impact of human interaction with robots, such as swearing at a robot nanny in front of our children or kicking a robot dog. But we can still ask ourselves what we think such behavior would say about us and what impact it could have on the humans observing it. Similarly, would we treat a robot that sorts packages and doesn't have a humanlike appearance any differently from a humanoid robot like Sophia?

If robots were accorded rights, how would they be enforced? Imagine taking a robot to court or an arbitration proceeding. Would the robot have its own human lawyer? Testify?

How we allocate responsibility for robots among the various stakeholders is a critical question: the companies manufacturing the robots, the companies and individuals who buy and use the robots, the regulators. The companies manufacturing and deploying robots with the public owe us transparency, an opportunity to grant our consent, and above all, safety.

I strongly oppose spending resources such as court time on metal machines when real people are deprived of desperately needed food, health care, and education. We have too far to go to guarantee human rights around the world before we get to robot rights.

This question reminds us that we may have to redraw lines in a world of increasingly blurred boundaries between humans and machines. Robot developers and experts should prevent machines and algorithms from achieving independent capacity to control or harm humans. I would flip this question instead to ask how we can assure that robots and other forms of AI cannot trample on our human rights. Technology should not redefine what it means to be human.

Chapter 5

Consumer Choices

Should we buy fast fashion?

The daughter of a close friend was giving away an extra-large Hefty trash bag with perfectly good clothes that still fit. My friend was shocked at the waste of money and materials. Yet the whole bag of inexpensive fast fashion clothes might have cost less than $100 at retail. What upset her was our throwaway mentality. An example: online British retailer Boohoo sold a bodycon minidress for £4 (around $5), about the cost of a vanilla spice latte at Starbucks in London (£3.75). According to the environmental organization Greenpeace, "In 1991, the average American bought 34 items of clothing each year. By 2007, they were buying 67 items every year." And only one quarter of those garments are later recycled.

What is fast fashion? One definition I came across calls it "landfill fashion." Fast fashion companies recreate high-fashion catwalk or runway trends and designs, and mass-produce them inexpensively. They are high volume, cheaply made, and designed to be quickly discarded. Sometimes fast fashion hits the stores almost before the models step off the catwalk. A fashionable knockoff that used to take six months can now be available to consumers in less than a week. The countermovement to it is sometimes called slow fashion—"mindful manufacturing . . . fair labor rights, natural materials, and lasting garments." Budget clothing, on the other hand, does not necessarily chase fashion trends, wear out, or even use synthetic materials so extensively.

Exploration

The guideposts of fast fashion appear to be short-termism, perpetuating our continuing addiction to new clothes and trends, a focus on revenues over principles, and a casual disregard for the environment.

Fast fashion companies may aim to make high-end designs more accessible for everyday consumers, but their approach to democratizing fashion comes at the cost of damage to the environment and exacerbating inequality. The UN Environment Program says that "it takes 3,781 liters of water to make one pair of jeans." According to a World Bank report, "The fashion industry is responsible for 10 percent of annual global carbon emissions—more than all international flights and maritime shipping combined." And that doesn't speak to the environmental impact of toxic chemicals and dyes, textile waste, water pollution, and pesticides.

Fast fashion also helps to foster what is known as planned obsolescence—designing clothes with an artificially limited useful life that need to be constantly replaced due to their poor quality and quickly outdated trendy fashion styles. It is the same concept smartphone manufacturers use to force expensive upgrades like changing the shape of the charger and using batteries that lose power quickly as they age.

We each have the power to buy or not buy disposable underpriced fashion clothing, as well as to seek quality (as well as other low-cost) brands. Or we can just purchase less, borrow and rent clothes from the companies now offering short-term rentals of designer clothing (renting an evening gown for a formal event), give away or sell our own used clothing, and seek out sustainable fabrics rather than environmentally dangerous synthetics. We can use social media to shift consumer discussions to a "less is more" culture (repurposing, sharing, handing down, re-cycling), moving from a throwaway culture that seeks out the latest fashion trends to searching for what lasts. Fast fashion retailers can't make money on what we don't buy.

But many stakeholders must contribute to reducing the impact of fast fashion and ensure a decent livelihood for fashion industry workers. Regulators should reinforce environmental impact standards; companies should offer more responsible budget clothing options.

Like fast food, I confess that I buy inexpensive fast fashion occasionally. The point is not to draw a line in the sand, or create feelings of guilt, but rather to consider how our purchasing power can help to influence and improve the choices companies make available to consumers, and improve company behavior.

Would you continue
to support a nonprofit
humanitarian organization
that pays an illegal bribe to
assure delivery of lifesaving
medical treatments?

You volunteer with, or donate to, a highly reputable nonprofit organization that provides medical services to people in developing countries in high-risk, dire situations. In fact, they are often the only organization providing health care in the aftermath of a natural disaster, pandemic, or other emergency. In order to deliver these lifesaving medications and vaccinations to one country following a major disease outbreak, the organization has to bribe government officials. The bureaucracy is rife with corruption, and these payments are so regularly required that they are almost considered a tax. The bribes do not represent a significant sum (relative to the organization's budget for the region); however, they are illegal under United States and local law. (Most exceptions from the law for de minimis payments such as gifts wouldn't apply when paying off government officials.) There is no indication of danger of any other misconduct that could harm the local population the organization serves. The local population has no other source of the supplies your organization can provide.

Exploration

Barring highly unusual circumstances, respecting the law is the minimum standard of ethics—usually a nonnegotiable baseline.

This question encourages us to look at the short-, medium-, and long-term consequences of our decisions *at the time of the decision.* When we see words like "life-threatening," our temptation is to leap to fix the short-term problem and put off considering longer-term risks and opportunities. One short-term consequence is both important and irreparable: the potential (avoidable) loss of life. Many people would pay a modest bribe to save lives and worry about the fallout later. I might opt to pay the bribe myself. But the medium- and long-term consequences here are also important and could ultimately cost lives as well. Whatever our decision on bribery, the conversation about longer-term consequences should be part and parcel of our thinking *now.*

So what are these potential consequences?

First, because the organization has broken the law, legal sanctions could follow. These sanctions might include preventing the organization from providing assistance to this country in the future to help others in need; accusations of bribery resulting in the dismissal of key staff; and jeopardizing the nonprofit's tax-exempt status, and their ability to offer tax deduction incentives as a way to encourage donations.

Second, donor trust can easily be lost. Donors don't expect bribery as a cost of doing business in treating patients. I don't know of any organizations that are transparent about bribery, whether as a general warning that it may be necessary or that it has been done. Annual reports show photos of employees caring for children, not slipping an envelope of cash to a uniformed customs officer. Today social media and cell phone cameras greatly increase the reputational risk of exposure.

Also, bribery that is systemic quickly becomes a habit, and sometimes the price escalates. One act of wrongdoing often begets another (what I call contagion and mutation of unethical behavior). The organization would face further ethical dilemmas—including whether to lie to the media, regulators, donors, beneficiaries, and even their own employees. Soon what seems like a single justifiable (if illegal) bribe becomes the organization's brand identity. And donors may flee over time, particularly given the competition for donor funding and the many needs in the world today.

Still, even with all these potential consequences over time, this is one situation that may call for the unpalatable and illegal option to bribe to save lives now. Critically, there don't seem to be alternatives. At the very least, the organization could be transparent about the *general* risks of bribery and corruption in the countries in which they work (as many corporations must disclose doing business in countries known for high levels of corruption in their documents to regulators and shareholders).

I always urge that we ask how the person the most adversely affected by our decision would feel. And then imagine that person is you: How would you feel if your own child's life were on the line?

Is purchasing organic food and products a more ethical choice?

When I was sheltering at home in northern California, grocery store runs were pretty much the only outing. Masked, sanitizer in hand, I confess to lingering longer than usual over the produce aisle and the ice cream freezer. I was struck by the increasing number of parallel options: organic peaches for $4 per pound, side by side with regular peaches for $2.35 per pound. From ice cream to chicken wings, organic products were everywhere . . . and they were considerably more expensive. I also learned that organic products need not be edible: I discovered organic body lotion and shampoo, makeup, textiles (wool, cotton), and pet foods.

Even where there were labels (cereal boxes, for example), I had no idea what my extra investment was bringing me—ethically or practically.

A quick primer on the definition of "organic":

The U.S. Department of Agriculture (USDA) says that for a food to be "USDA certified organic" it must be "grown and processed according to federal guidelines addressing, among many factors, soil quality, animal raising practices, pest and weed control, and use of additives." The USDA categorizes organic products as: *100 percent organic* (all ingredients must be organic); *organic* (must contain 95 percent or more organic ingredients); and *made with organic ingredients* (must contain at least 70 percent organic ingredients, and cannot display the USDA organic seal). That said, customers (like me!) often see the *made with organic ingredients* label, and don't understand the USDA distinctions.

Exploration

In 2020, organic food sales in the U.S. surged by 12.4 percent to $61.9 billion.

On the one hand, a 2012 in-depth study from Stanford University's Center for Health Policy determined on average, organic foods were no more nutritious than their cheaper, nonorganic counterparts. On the other hand, organic farming *is* widely considered more sustainable, as it uses natural rather than synthetic pesticides. "The . . . wider variety of plants enhances biodiversity and results in better soil quality and reduced pollution," according to the Columbia University Climate School.

While buying organic may contribute to a more ethical food system, I do not view deciding not to buy organic as necessarily a lapse in ethics. Given the choice between consuming more fruits, vegetables, and proteins that are not grown organically, and purchasing fewer of these healthy foods in order to eat more expensive organic foods, I would choose the former. Also, because organic foods do not contain preservatives they often do not keep as long.

For those who can afford it, I do see Princeton University philosopher Peter Singer's point that buying organic is the better ethical choice because our food purchases contribute to a vast global industry with impact on animals, farmers, the environment, and future generations.

Organic purchases are one of many alternatives proactively to do good and reinforce our commitment to an ethical food supply. But there are many other ways to contribute to the community, the environment, and tackling inequality. Some experts suggest reducing the amount of meat in one's diet, reducing food waste, avoiding chemically processed foods, and paying attention to local sourcing. Check the information on the package or offered by the store about specific products to see if your highest priorities are being met (for some it may mean no artificial colors or sweeteners or organically raised animals).

To me, organic food is sometimes synonymous with luxury ethics. And unlike luxury clothing, we need food to live—so many people are struggling to feed their families, including those who have lost their jobs because of the Covid-19 pandemic. Twenty-five thousand people die of starvation throughout the world every day. In terms of food priorities, it seems to me that we should first ensure that the millions of people who are hungry in and outside the U.S. receive nutritious food before we call out people for not buying organic.

What are the steps to recovery from an ethics mishap?

n December 2015, a 2014 working paper from Harvard Business School that found widespread discrimination on Airbnb's platform was reported in the media. The researchers claimed that Airbnb's platform encouraged racial profiling because hosts were able to view a prospective guest's picture and personal details before deciding whether to accept or deny requests. The paper concluded that renters with "distinctively African American names" were 16 percent less likely to be accepted by hosts compared to renters with "distinctively white names." Racial discrimination had been a known concern on the internet and was prohibited in the hospitality industry (including through the Civil Rights Act of 1964, which specifically prohibits "discrimination or segregation on the ground of race, color, religion, or national origin").

Airbnb was a blend of the internet and hospitality, on a technology platform that matches hosts and guests and that could only supercharge the risk of racism. In addition, Airbnb hosts were offering a blend of hotel stay (where discrimination is illegal) and private home (where discrimination is abhorrent but often legal). No one had determined what the law was in this new blended business model, but the ethics were clear. To their credit, the leaders of Airbnb took full responsibility. Brian Chesky, cofounder and CEO of Airbnb, acknowledged, "There were lots of things we didn't think about when we, as three white guys, designed the platform." Airbnb also took a number of comprehensive antidiscrimination steps, calling discrimination "the greatest challenge we face as a company." As Chesky said, "Our real innovation . . . is designing a framework to allow millions of people to trust one another . . . We intend to do everything possible to learn from these incidents when they occur."

Exploration

Every one of us makes mistakes. And we are all called on to respond to the mistakes of others.

In either case, ethical resilience and recovery requires three steps: telling the truth (to ourselves and others), owning our part of the responsibility, and committing to a plan of repair and prevention of future mishaps. All require a hefty dose of humility. All, I believe, rest on the late poet, memoirist, and civil rights activist Maya Angelou's famous advice: "Do the best you can until you know better. Then when you know better, do better."

Let's start with *knowing*. Start by asking whether you have the information you need in order to understand how to react to your own or someone else's error. Information is another way of gauging reality: a truthful assessment of what happened, why it happened, and what drove any spread of the regrettable behavior.

Information requires considering what *could* happen, not just what will happen when we make choices. Looking back, the same applies: what *could have* happened, not just what did happen. Just because we got away with a poor choice doesn't mean we don't face ethical recovery. Try to imagine the effect on people you will never meet—for example, the potential victims if you realize you have Covid-19 symptoms, decide not to self-isolate, and seriously infect another person or persons.

Identify the missing information (*the gap*), and the reason for it. Consider these scenarios:

- We had the information we needed but disregarded it and forged ahead anyway.

- We should have, or could have, had the information we needed, but didn't seek it out or use it.

- We couldn't have had the information we needed and made the best possible decision under the circumstances—and clarified the gaps in information to monitor events and behavior going forward.

Check for some common traps. Did you miss something that was right in front of you (as was the case with Airbnb)—which happens to us all? Did you make assumptions: base your decision on gut reactions, instinct, "everyone says," "I saw it on social media," or "the last time *X* happened, so I expected the same thing to happen again"? Did you wait for information to come to you rather than proactively seeking it out? Did you neglect to monitor changing information?

Now for the *doing*. The goal is to put your principles into action based on what you now know. Airbnb implemented a range of fixes, from removing the requirement to post customer photos, to new antidiscrimination policies, to denying hosts exhibiting racist behavior access to the platform. They have continued to monitor progress and consider further adjustments and changing information.

We can all strive to *know* better, and then when we do, *do* better—and honor others' efforts to do the same—with empathy and humility.

Are there ethical reasons that would persuade you to consider becoming a vegan?

A friend of mine who is the president of a California university noted that their dining halls are trying to nudge students toward plant-based choices in their diet, rather than emphasize options that feature beef, pork, fish, or chicken. Their view seems to be that vegan dishes are healthier for students or that vegan dishes are more sustainable food choices for the environment—or both. My own students are questioning their food choices as well.

The *Cambridge English Dictionary* defines veganism as "the practice of not eating or using animal products, such as meat, fish, eggs, cheese, or leather." An "ethical vegan" is someone who not only follows a vegan diet, but who also lives by the philosophy that animals should not be exploited for food, clothing, or other uses. According to the Vegan Society, the oldest vegan organization in the world, the ethical vegan avoids products tested on animals, and use of animals for sports or entertainment (such as racing), clothing and accessories, and makeup and personal hygiene items.

Exploration

Some people choose to be vegan or vegetarian for reasons of health, parenting, the environment, concern for animal welfare, or for other considerations. I focus here on the view of many vegans that it is morally wrong to consume animal products.

The *Stanford Encyclopedia of Philosophy* identifies a range of reasons that producing and consuming meat can be seen as morally wrong: it causes harm to the environment (veganism reduces our carbon footprint); industrial farming consumes vast quantities of water and energy, and produces enormous amounts of waste that must be treated and disposed of; it causes animals unnecessary pain (because of the conditions they're kept in); and it results in the unnecessary killing of animals (because we have other food options).

Exploring moral veganism presents an opportunity to banish "all or nothing" thinking. Taking partial steps toward veganism—such as eating vegan dishes several days a week—is better than taking no steps at all. Every choice matters. For example, Princeton philosophy professor and author Peter Singer calls himself a "flexible vegan," who allows himself to eat vegetarian when traveling. I agree that making some helpful choices is better than making none.

Put differently, even occasional vegans can do tremendous good by advocating for good choices rather than absolutes. Perfection is one of the most insidious drivers of the spread of unethical behavior. It is neither a laudable goal nor an achievable one and can trigger other forms of unethical behavior, like overstating the environmental impact of consuming meat, reducing the food supply for those in need, or lying about our eating habits.

Ethical veganism can also spotlight a decision-by-decision approach to ethics and allow us to evaluate choices, not stances. We're not condemning those who are not vegans, but rather choosing to praise the choices that make a better world for all of us. Veganism can prompt us to consider alternative ways to achieve common goals by creating better living conditions for livestock, reducing the amount of meat we consume that has the highest environmental impact, finding ways to reduce waste, and improving our diets. (All science and health matters should be based on expert advice.) There are many ways to reach these goals, and they don't all involve becoming vegan.

Ethical vegans help us connect to our own ethical principles and the identity they reflect—whether or not we are vegans. You and I might or might not wish to become vegans, or follow their practices, but I will learn from their choices, and become more informed and ethically resilient as a result.

Would you fly on a
Boeing 737 Max plane?

I was grappling with whether my family should fly on Boeing planes. Here's why: In November 2020, the Federal Aviation Administration (FAA) rescinded the order grounding Boeing's 737 Max 8 and 9 planes that was issued in 2019 following two fatal crashes within a five-month period in Indonesia and Ethiopia. Disturbingly, Boeing knew that the software on its 737 Max planes—the Maneuvering Characteristics Augmentation System, or MCAS—was faulty. But they decided to wait years to fix it. And after the second crash, then CEO Dennis Muilenburg personally called President Trump to urge him to keep the Boeing 737 Max planes in the air, after sixty-five other nations decided to ground them. President Trump refused.

The ethics failure behind the crashes involves a complex history of poor decisions by Boeing executives and engineers, and regulators. The crux: first, due to competition from Airbus, Boeing ditched plans to build a new fuel-efficient passenger jet and instead redesigned the old 737 (first launched in 1967) with fuel-saving engines. Putting heavy new engines on the old plane changed the 737 Max's aerodynamics. The fix: the anti-stall software called

MCAS. Boeing made a pivotal decision that a single alert from one of its two sensors in the nose of the plane was enough, rather than relying on a second sensor alert as a fail-safe—an essential in an industry where redundancy is the key to safety. Another serious error involved Boeing's missing that a critical safety alert system to counter the risk of a faulty sensor was tied to an indicator that was a premium option (like luxury seating) rather than a mandatory feature. And Boeing did not notify customers or pilots about the need for the fix. In addition, Boeing cut corners with pilot training and testing. Meanwhile, the FAA gave Boeing increasing authority over its own safety certification process, thereby undermining the governmental independence of the review.

In rescinding the grounding of the planes, the FAA cited improvements in design and ordered operators to "meet all other applicable requirements, such as completing new training for pilots and conducting maintenance activity" before returning the planes to service.

Exploration

The question is when and under what circumstances passengers will be comfortable that Boeing has remedied the company's ethics failures enough to earn their trust to fly again on a 737 Max plane.

This is not a situation in which there are a few rogue individuals who can be fired (a CEO committing fraud), or where the flawed ethics don't affect consumers directly. This is the worst of all worlds: unpredictable ethics risks throughout the organization becoming life-threatening events for customers and employees. Worse, the then CEO did not prioritize passenger safety and perspective with his decisions that followed the accidents.

Ethical resilience and recovery require taking full responsibility for the mistakes and the underlying causes, then being transparent and having a plan going forward. Muilenburg ducked responsibility, suggesting after the two crashes that "procedures were not completely followed" by the pilots—in other words, the pilots, not Boeing, were to blame.

Ethics and safety are inextricably intertwined. Boeing did not just have a software problem, triggering tragic consequences that spread throughout the organization, to passengers, their families, the FAA, and the global airline industry. The company was mired in an uncontrollable contagion of failed ethics throughout Boeing affecting all stakeholders. The new CEO, David Calhoun, admitted that fixing Boeing was "more than I imagined it would be, honestly. And it speaks to the weaknesses of our leadership." He would later say, "The objective is to get the Max up safely. Period." The key lesson: We cannot just address the technical wrongdoing, insufficient training, and internal and external oversight failures. Genuine recovery—ethically and in terms of safety—requires identifying and eradicating all the *drivers* of the behavior that caused these tragedies to happen and be repeated. *Until we do, those same drivers will trigger other dangerous behaviors.*

Some of the causes of spreading unethical behavior at

play here include: competition and greed, fear (of losing business, as well as employees' fear of speaking up), impunity and failed regulatory oversight (the FAA's reliance on Boeing to control too much in self-certification), and weak leadership. All are exacerbated after the severe drop in business due to Covid-19.

Every one of these causes could affect the safety, security practices, and the oversight of *all Boeing planes*, not just the 737 Max. The ethics lapses in decision making cannot be limited to one product.

What other financial shortcuts did Boeing take that might not have surfaced yet? Are there other pilots flying without adequate training (no fault of the pilots)? How exactly did the FAA fix the *decision and regulatory oversight process*? Has Boeing shored up its decision making and manufacturing processes throughout the organization to regain our trust?

As consumers, we often don't have a choice of what plane we fly on. This question shows us how much we rely on other stakeholders, particularly regulators and the airlines that purchase and deploy Boeing planes, to assure ethical oversight of all aspects of travel.

Should you stop donating to a nonprofit organization if you find out about a sexual misconduct scandal?

The headlines can be deeply disturbing. "Sexual misconduct and management cover-up at humanitarian charity." "Government bans nonprofit organizations after claims of sexual misconduct." "NGO workers hired local prostitutes." "Well-intentioned employees pushed out after reporting allegations of sexual exploitation."

The headlines above are composites of headlines from around the world revealing sexual misconduct at nonprofit organizations of all sizes, missions, and locations—anonymized to avoid spotlighting any one organization.

In this question, I have also anonymized examples of the kind of horrific behavior that has come to light, to avoid targeting any one organization. Top of mind are instances of nonprofit employees pressuring beneficiaries (or their family or community members) for sex in exchange for desperately needed food, medicines, or other assistance. The abuse of power is particularly egregious in times of crisis—a pandemic, in the aftermath of a natural disaster, in a conflict zone. Misconduct can be more difficult to detect when employees and volunteers serve far from home; local laws and customs may be (wrongly) used as excuses for unacceptable behavior.

Exploration

All the global NGOs and other nonprofit organizations I have advised, researched, volunteered for, or donated to—and their peer organizations—have had some episodes of sexual misconduct. No organization in any sector can boast a spotless past, or guarantee a stainless future. That said, the overwhelming majority of employees at nonprofits work with impeccable integrity in terribly hard conditions, often for reduced pay—providing lifesaving assistance that would not otherwise be available.

This question pits our hearts—compassion for people in need and admiration for the good work done by nonprofit organizations—against our repugnance at sexual misconduct. While this is not a question that affects most of us directly, through our donations and volunteering we have considerable power to affect the organization and the people it serves.

Sexual misconduct is one of the most virulently contagious forms of unethical behavior there is.

People receiving aid in crisis situations often have no other source of aid (giving nonprofit workers enormously greater power). Add to that impunity (conduct undetected or unpunished), information silos, arrogance, greed (or just financial pressure), cultural pressure (blaming women for an assault), and failed compliance systems. Moreover, victims may be unable to report transgressions due to language barriers, fear and shaming, or overly complicated reporting systems.

No organization can prevent all misconduct. But here are some questions you can ask to make an ethically informed choice: Did the organization investigate the scandal to determine the full scope of the problem (ideally with independent investigators)? Was the organization transparent with the public and donors as information came to light?

Did they then fix both the specific challenges (firing guilty individuals for cause) and systemic aspects of the problem (buttressing organization-wide compliance, more thoroughly vetting candidates when hiring, simplifying reporting processes)?

All of this can be difficult in nonprofit organizations with limited budgets, particularly those operating in many different countries with local customs and laws. Is the organization current with best practices? What precautions does the organization take to protect the most vulnerable (children, the elderly, the infirm, or those who have no other sources of life-critical health services)?

If you can answer yes—or they're working toward yes—to these questions, I would consider continuing support.

A few red flags might convince us to give our money elsewhere, such as a pattern of resorting to bribery to gain access, repeated failure to use donor funds for the specified purposes, failing to fire the perpetrators, or violation of medical ethics.

If you feel you need to withdraw support because the organization is just not handling the misconduct properly, tell them why you made the decision. And consider finding an alternative way to support the people the organization partners with and serves.

Should we buy clothing from companies that don't treat the people who work for them properly?

On April 23, 2013, deep cracks and fissures were discovered in the foundation walls of the Rana Plaza building in Bangladesh's Dhaka District, where thousands in the garment industry labored making clothes. Workers were reassured the building was safe and were told to return to their jobs the next morning. That afternoon, on April 24, the building collapsed and over 1,100 people were buried in the rubble; thousands more were injured. It was the deadliest garment factory disaster in history. "Soldiers, paramilitary police officers, firefighters and other citizens clawed through the wreckage, searching for survivors and bodies," reported the *New York Times*.

The factories housed in the Rana Plaza produced clothing for many Western fashion leaders. An investigation found that the building violated building codes; in fact, the top four floors had been built illegally without any permits at all. Scott Nova, executive director of Worker Rights Consortium (an independent labor rights monitoring organization), said in the aftermath, "The price pressure these buyers put on factories undermines any prospect that factories will undertake the costly repairs and renovations that are necessary to make these buildings safe." A spokesperson for one major brand, after expressing sympathy for the victims, said they were "committed" to urging stronger safety guidelines.

Exploration

This tragic event and similar stories ask us to decide whether, as consumers, we will stop purchasing from companies that don't guarantee decent working conditions throughout their supply chain—even if it means paying a few dollars more for (or going without) the product. There is a hidden cost many of us are unaware of to the $2 T-shirts we buy from discount stores, and even the promotions high-end retailers offer.

This isn't an instance where the products themselves are dangerous to consumers (like toxic baby powder), or an isolated case of wrongdoing (like sexual harassment by a senior leader). Rather, the ethics of these companies' entire *business models* are in question.

When buying clothing or other goods, none of us is perfect in considering our principles, such as safety, integrity, equality, and dignity. And many people do not have the means to have much choice when purchasing clothes. But many of us don't think about how easy it would be to live without these goods, find them elsewhere, or forgo a latte or two to pay a bit more.

Applying those principles is not so easy. What if our (or the company's) principles are in conflict? Women working in these factories depend on their wages to support their families. Many hardworking consumers simply don't have the extra few dollars. Would taking our business elsewhere hurt these people?

The ethical solution is not simply a factory closure or retail price increase—or our decision as consumers.

Companies can trim costs elsewhere, such as with executive compensation and perks. And they can eliminate products that just don't make sense when linking cost to humane business practices.

My own view is that companies are responsible for the ethics of every link in their supply chain. They can outsource everything from textile purchasing to contract negotiation, but *they cannot outsource their ethical responsibility.* Some companies claim they can't know everything because the supply chain is so complex or so long. My response: yes they can. Part of the challenge in monitoring the safety and well-being of "workers has been the difficulty of holding each party in the supply chain accountable"—the companies, people, resources, and distributors who turn raw materials into a finished product. One factory at Rana Plaza was making clothes without the retailer's knowledge, because the work had been subcontracted out by a wholesaler. But for companies it's a question of priorities, financial investment, and effort. The companies linked to the Rana Plaza tragedy could have, and should have, known about the unsafe working conditions.

We also need greater industry-wide transparency of company practices—like nutrition labels in the food industry—that clearly specify where products are made and a simplified certification of minimum standards. We need enhanced regulation and global advocacy.

Our individual purchasing decisions matter—in the case of retail goods, they can influence people we may never meet. They reflect our ethics, and they contribute to society's ethics.

Refusing to buy from brands that mistreat their workers is one option among so many ways to contribute to a solution, including speaking out, signing an online petition, and donating to nonprofit organizations that help people in these countries in need.

Should tax preparation for individual tax returns be free?

n 2002, the George W. Bush administration proposed that the Internal Revenue Service (IRS) create a free online filing option for taxpayers. But the tax preparation industry, concerned about their profits, negotiated a compromise: companies would offer complimentary versions of their software, through a multiyear agreement between the IRS and the Free File Alliance, providing "free and secure online tax return preparation and filing services" to low- to moderate-income filers (those who generally earn $72,000 or less, although some tax companies have lower income limits). Their goal was to provide 60 percent or more of taxpayers with free online filing.

While more than 60 million returns have been filed since the program began in 2003, according to the alliance's website, the annual number of taxpayers using the free software dropped from 5 million in 2003 to half of that in 2020. Although 100 million Americans are eligible to use the free software, the Free File Alliance executive director reports, less than 3 million do so. According to interviews conducted with former employees of Intuit and H&R Block, their companies actively steer people away from the free services, and try to turn them into paying customers. H&R Block dropped out of the alliance in 2020. And in July 2021, Intuit, the maker of TurboTax, announced they would no longer be a part of the alliance.

Exploration

Paying taxes is a civic duty. It's also the law. The system for doing so should be accessible to all: easy to use, free of charge for basic returns, available on mobile devices, verifiable, and with access to a human in the loop to help where necessary.

Some countries such as Britain and Japan don't require taxpayers to file tax returns—the government just "withholds taxes from wage income and handles the paperwork." (Those with more complicated finances still need to file.) In 2006, Austan Goolsbee, who later served as chairman of President Obama's Council of Economic Advisers, suggested the idea of the "simple return," in which taxpayers review and sign off on already completed tax forms.

This question spotlights what appears to be an ethically charged uneven battle between the federal government and commercial tax prep providers, ensnaring average citizens just trying to pay taxes in a timely fashion in the cross fire.

With the Free File Alliance founded in 2003, the government created a monopoly that hadn't existed before. As a result of the alliance, the IRS agreed not to compete in providing free online services to taxpayers. Imagine if we had to go through private companies to receive Social Security checks. A series of exposés by ProPublica revealed that "free" often involved a series of paid enticements to purchase upgrades and additional assistance, playing on customers' fears to drive the tax preparation companies' growth despite the free service. And "free" applies to federal tax returns. Each company in the alliance was only required to cover 10 percent of taxpayers, so companies could manage their customer selection to keep their most lucrative customers. In my view, the system seems to rest on a quagmire of lobbyists, corporate advertising, social media strategy, and sophisticated product design, with respect to a fundamental civic duty that every American must fulfill.

The Free File Alliance argues that the tax collector—the IRS—should not also be the tax preparer. Doing both creates a conflict of interest.

Ethics must be made easy: the default option should not be an obstacle course. This is particularly crucial for anything involving citizenship—it applies to everything from obtaining Covid-19 vaccinations and voting to recycling and being able to report drunk drivers. If the federal government cannot dedicate the resources to a government-run free filing system, regulators should consider other ethics protections: eliminate the filing process for millions of Americans in lower income groups; ban the manipulative tactics used to steer consumers to paid tax preparation software; and require the companies in the Free File Alliance to display the free option prominently on websites, in Google searches, and in advertising. Governments have a responsibility to support well-intentioned citizens in efficiently and effectively complying with tax law by mitigating the risks that unnecessary government bureaucracy and the proliferation of for-profit intermediaries may pose to performing civic duties.

Should I switch my giving in response to Covid-19 or other emergencies?

Consider a situation in which you have decided you want to give money to your favorite charity—an animal adoption program, because you love animals. And your roommate or partner or best friend jumps in and takes you to task. How can you give money to animals, they argue, when people are dying from the Covid-19 pandemic, and millions are out of work and are struggling to get by? A lecture continues about how it doesn't matter whether you feel most connected to organizations that some would say aren't society's highest priority—a ballet program for underprivileged children or a neighborhood playground— we all should give to issues like supporting the victims of Covid-19, climate change, undernourished children, or the toxic lead in the water supply of Flint, Michigan.

The word "philanthropy" comes from the ancient Greek phrase "love of humankind." In 1835, when French civil servant Alexis de Tocqueville published the first volume of his famous work *Democracy in America*, he admired the American penchant for forming "associations"—coming together as citizens through nonprofit organizations that strengthened our social bonds and supported one another. Today, many of us include in our giving to others our time, our experience and talent, material goods, financial support, even our support in social and mainstream media.

Exploration

Charitable giving is a deeply personal decision. You don't owe anyone an explanation of how much and where you give, any more than you owe them an explanation of what is in your grocery cart or your Netflix selection. Only you can decide where you feel you can do the most good, have the greatest connection, and maximize your giving capacity (whether you are giving your time, your expertise, or your money).

Here are a few questions that can help you anchor your giving with ethics in mind. Ask yourself, Does the organization demonstrate a commitment to ethics essentials regardless of the mission? For example, are they transparent (telling you when things go wrong)? Do they fight discrimination and inequality? Do they hold themselves accountable for what they do and how they do it? Do they focus on *outcomes* (children acquiring skills) rather than actions (providing school books)?

When do you give? Perhaps during the pandemic you decided to continue to give to food banks, but chose those hit particularly hard by Covid-19. Or, alternatively, you decided to remain loyal to your favorite arts organization, which you realized will need help to restart when the pandemic subsides. Maybe this year you cannot afford to give money at all, but you help deliver food or medication to a neighbor who can't go out.

Will your gift make a difference? Médecins Sans Frontières/Doctors Without Borders (for which I have served on the U.S. advisory board for years) used to have a campaign called "a franc a day" (before the franc was replaced by the euro). A river of collective generosity from people from all walks of life became the bedrock of the Nobel Peace Prize–winning organization, even as individuals came and went. Other organizations are set up for only large donations. Effective altruism—a field of study using evidence and reasoning to try to do as much good as possible with available resources—is another lens for considering giving.

Lifting us all up and creating a compassionate society requires a complex tapestry of sustained efforts to support individuals and organizations—to further generosity and grateful assistance. As one chief executive of a global NGO said to me in 2020, given the nature of the Covid-19 pandemic and its resulting shrapnel, everything will be about, or at least touched by, Covid-19 for the foreseeable future. Organizations faced increased pressure and costs to protect staff and find alternative ways to serve beneficiaries. Many will face reduced donations because donors devoted more funds to address the impact of Covid-19; many donors may not have the capacity to continue giving at their previous levels.

Giving—in whatever way you give—should be a moment of joy, celebration, and gratitude that we are in a position to give, whatever and wherever and however you give.

Does buying (or not buying) a disposable plastic bottle of water really make a difference?

You have been on a hike and at the end you are very thirsty. But the convenience store at the trailhead doesn't have a water fountain. The only water available is sold in individual plastic bottles. You care deeply about the environment, and you are dismayed at the thought of purchasing a plastic water bottle, even if you dispose of it in a recycling bin. But you need water. Or perhaps you slipped up and forgot to bring your reusable water container to a concert or an outing, and resort to purchasing a bottle of water only to be confronted by a friend, family member, or colleague as they fix you with a withering stare. I have found myself in many such situations and bought the bottle.

Exploration

Many of us wonder whether, particularly without data, our one small decision will have an impact. In the case of plastic bottles, the data is striking. *National Geographic* reports that globally, "more than a million plastic bottles are sold every single minute." Further, "in the U.S., only 30% of these bottles are recycled." A single plastic bottle takes "about 450 years" to decompose. And plastic bottles are the third-most collected plastic trash in the Ocean Conservancy's annual international beach cleanup.

The ethics of our individual decisions matter because the small stuff adds up, especially when repeated by ourselves and others. They become habits that persist and spread among friends, within offices, across towns, on social media. Ethics contagion can be either positive or negative. For example, in offices that provide water fountains or sinks, few would *think* of displaying a plastic bottle on their desk.

There will be occasions when there are no alternatives. Sometimes there just doesn't seem to be another option to bottled water at an airport or at a concert. And there are places in the world where tap water isn't safe, and cheap plastic water bottles are the only affordable option. (Hopefully corporations that supply potable water will offer better choices. Bottled water is roughly 2,000 times more expensive than the equivalent amount of tap water, according to the American Water Works Association.)

My suggestion is to look for *additional* strategies rather than a license for a pass. Avoiding buying water in plastic bottles where possible is important, but we should also pursue a range of other measures, such as voting for tax credits for people and companies that recycle; educating our community about recycling; and using stainless steel reusable water bottles. And the water will be healthier (avoiding bisphenol A—or BPA—used in the manufacture of plastic bottles and linked to various health hazards).

Ultimately, our actions, no matter how small, make a difference.

Similarly, seeing the ethics opportunity in a single plastic water bottle can change our and others' individual and collective impacts on the world about many other issues, bottle by bottle, with seemingly little effort. I know I need to do better.

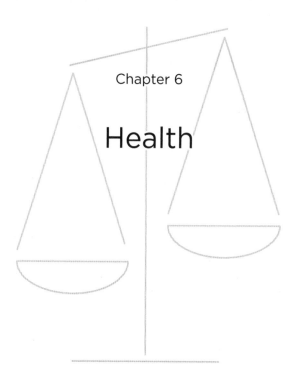

Chapter 6

Health

Should organ donation be opt-in or opt-out, from an ethical perspective?

As of this writing, 106,822 people in the U.S. were waiting for organs, and 17 people died waiting each day. Organ donation, as described by the Cleveland Clinic, is "the process of surgically removing an organ . . . from one person (the organ donor) and placing it into another person (the recipient)." Organs can be donated by living donors, as well as by deceased donors. There were 7,397 living donors in the U.S. in 2019, and 11,870 deceased donors according to the United Network for Organ Sharing (the nonprofit organization that manages the U.S. transplantation system). A single donor can supply organs for as many as eight different recipients.

Ninety percent of people in America favor organ donation, but only 60 percent actually sign up. Currently in the U.S., each of us has to actively register to donate our organs, in what is known as the opt-in or explicit consent system. The alternative is what is known as the opt-out system, where the government automatically enrolls individuals as organ donors, unless the individual has specifically selected not to donate their organs. The change in the default decision can make a significant difference. Germany, like the U.S., uses an opt-in system, and donation rates hover at 12 percent. Neighboring Austria, with a similar culture and economy, uses opt-out, and has a donation rate of 99.98 percent.

Exploration

Organ donation literally touches the core of our physical and spiritual selves. Among the stakeholders in organ donation are the organ donor, their family, the organ recipient and their family and loved ones, doctors, our spiritual advisors, and the general public.

As a society, our goal is to increase the number of organs available for transplant, by increasing organ donation. One way to do that is to shift the laws from an opt-in system where the individual must specifically request that their organs be donated, to an opt-out system. Twenty countries in the European Union, as well as Great Britain, have some form of opt-out system.

Switching to an opt-out system, however, while effective in increasing the supply of available organs for transplants, must rest on a foundation of robust transparency—making sure that the public understands what is at stake for them and offering a simple way to opt out if they wish. Our informed consent is not truly informed without both. Finally, ethics require monitoring—periodically notifying people who have, or have not, opted out—as our thinking on our decisions can change over time.

Complex ethical decisions benefit from looking for alternatives as well. The state of Illinois adopted in 2006 a policy of *mandated choice*, which required people applying for a driver's license to answer the "yes or no" question, "Do you wish to be an Organ Donor?" It is your choice, but you must make a choice.

Another potential solution is to offer tax incentives—a carrot, versus a stick—to those who donate an organ. But paying for organs is fraught with ethics risks. Educating the public about the importance of organ donation can also be effective and increase transparency.

Organ donation has a life-critical impact on another human being and their loved ones, in a way that most of the decisions we make may not. For some, the decision not to donate their organs is a matter of faith or religion. For others, it is an extraordinary opportunity to save or dramatically improve lives. Whatever our views, organ donation should be the result of a thoughtful decision, not something thrust upon us without choice.

As a society, our principles, policies, and practices say a great deal about how we balance individual autonomy versus saving lives.

Are you ethically obligated to tell your children if you have an inheritable disease?

The facts were unusual, but the case highlighted a life-critical decision that we are increasingly finding ourselves having to make. A woman in the U.K., known to the public only as ABC to preserve her confidentiality, sued NHS Trust, a group within the National Health Service in the U.K., for not informing her that her father had Huntington's disease. Huntington's is at present an incurable, inheritable degenerative brain disease. Symptoms, according to the Mayo Clinic, can include difficulty walking, difficulty speaking, tremors, depression, problems with impulse control, and bipolar disorder and other cognitive and psychiatric disorders.

With Huntington's disease, children have a 50/50 chance of inheriting the genetic mutation that causes the disease. Those with the mutation develop the disease. About 30,000 people in the U.S. have Huntington's disease, with another 200,000 at risk of developing it, including ABC, who ultimately tested positive for the genetic mutation.

Exploration

This story zeroes in on the gut-wrenching ethical quandaries behind a parent's decision on whether to tell their child and other family members that they have an inheritable disease—regardless of the parent's doctor's confidentiality obligations. Today, with increased genetic testing, including direct-to-consumer (DTC) genetic testing kits like 23andMe, we have the unprecedented ability to discover whether we have a predisposition for a genetically inheritable disease, without even consulting a doctor. The information discovered using DTC kits often affects others and varies significantly depending on one's situation, including the nature of the disease, family circumstances, the ages of the individuals most directly affected, and other factors.

This question puts many ethical considerations—health, honesty, courage, compassion, autonomy—in conflict with others that are also important, like privacy and confidentiality. At its core, this situation hinges on the most powerful force in ethics: truth. By truth, I mean the right to know, but also the right not to be burdened by knowledge that you can't un-know.

First, consider the rights of others who potentially need to be told. At the very top of the list are those who could inherit the disease (children and their children) and their parents if the children are minors. I would allow an adult child to make the decision about whether to tell their partner, spouse, family members, or others who might need to care for them. No one who is not directly affected needs to be told. Extenuating circumstances like mental health issues should also be considered.

If a parent doesn't tell their adult child, the child loses the power to make life-critical choices for themselves. That includes the ability to seek medical help and the decision to have children—and their choice to tell or not tell their own loved ones.

The father in the scenario robbed his daughter of the opportunity to decide whether to have a child. He valued his own privacy at the cost of his daughter's right to know.

Parents may wish to shield a child who is under the age of eighteen from this information so as not to burden them before they are emotionally ready, particularly if telling them wouldn't alter the choices available or the disease often presents in adulthood.

This question puts all involved in an impossible situation. The decision not to tell is so much more than a stand-alone decision: it effectively results in the parent controlling a series of follow-on decisions that are not theirs to make. The best you can do may be to consider the principles raised above, and what you would want done if you were in their shoes. Consider as well what you would think about what you did, looking back on your choice in the future. Ideally, we should consider how we might face these questions prior to using DTC kits. And as a society we will need to reflect on the implications of doctor-patient confidentiality obligations in this new world in which our own health care testing may reveal unprecedented information about the health of others.

What are the ethical considerations behind informed consent?

Henrietta Lacks, the subject of Rebecca Skloot's critically acclaimed book *The Immortal Life of Henrietta Lacks*, was a Black woman treated for cervical cancer when she was thirty-one years old at the Johns Hopkins Hospital in 1951. Lacks died, but her tissue and cells, harvested for research without her knowledge or consent, continue to live on. They became the first human cells successfully grown in a laboratory setting. Named HeLa cells (after the first two letters in Lacks's names), they were shared "freely and widely for scientific research," because her cells were found to be durable and prolific. Those HeLa cells have led to countless medical breakthroughs, from the polio and Covid-19 vaccines to AIDS research to cancer treatments.

Informed consent, one of the three pillars that support ethical decision making (along with transparency and effective listening), means agreeing to an action based on an understanding of the action and its consequences.

Exploration

Henrietta Lacks's story continues to raise disturbing questions about who controls the cells taken from a patient's body. This ethical dilemma emerges in procedures as varied as tonsil removal and the whisking away of a placenta after birth, to skin cells obtained through a biopsy. Too often consent really means "do it our way or we'll show you the highway." One hospital consent form I obtained stated, "I consent to the taking of pictures, videotapes or other electronic reproductions of the patient's medical or surgical condition or treatment . . . consistent with the Hospital's mission, such as education and research." Agree to the expansive terms or you can't get a medically necessary procedure. It's one thing to click "I agree" and skip the fine print on the Apple Music terms of service. It's quite another when it comes to our bodies. In either case, we don't actually have a choice.

Some believe such medical consent contributes to the good of society; others are concerned with the right to decide for yourself what happens to your tissues. Skloot, in a *New York Times* op-ed, highlights diverging views: "Some believe their souls live on in the disembodied cells," some feel "it's unethical not to use [these cells] to advance science," and others "worry that genetic information will be linked to them . . . in harmful or discriminatory ways—particularly minorities."

I want to banish "sign or you can't have a procedure" *binary thinking* about the ethics of our decisions. So how can we obtain genuine consent to maximize the good for society, and minimize the risk to privacy and more? One way to do that is for health care providers to make elements unrelated to the procedure (the "extras") *opt-in*. Here are examples you might not even notice if, like me, you felt too nervous about a procedure to read the fine print.

We should not be required to allow the hospital to sell or share our tissues (or videotapes and photos of our treatments) with *commercial third parties*.

The consent form could add a commitment to *data privacy* and add ironclad anonymity (although increasingly there is technology to reverse anonymity).

The form's reference to the "potential for overlapping surgery" (your doctor could leave the operating room and perform another operation somewhere else if needed . . . leaving you in the hands of another "qualified physician") should be limited to exceptional cases.

The form I obtained required the physician to "explain" the procedure and risks and benefits "to [your] satisfaction." This information should include not only everything that will be done, but why, the pros and cons, the *alternatives*, and the potential consequences. It's unlikely that institutions will change, but we can protect ourselves by forcing medical providers to take the time to explain until we feel we understand our choices.

The bottom line: if the consent form is overly broad, and we can't choose from a menu of options, we have no choice at all.

Would you tell someone who is suffering from dementia when a close relative has died?

Your mother, who suffers from late-stage dementia, lives in a nursing home. (The most common form of progressive dementia, according to the World Health Organization, is Alzheimer's, which may account for 60 to 80 percent of cases. The World Health Organization defines dementia as a "deterioration in cognitive function beyond what might be expected from the usual consequences of biological aging.") She is no longer able to care for herself. A close relative—a daughter or son, a brother or sister, her spouse or partner—dies. Do you tell her? While she has occasional moments of lucidity, her short-term memory is poor, and she struggles to recognize family when they visit.

If you do decide to tell her, you need to think about how much detail you share. On the other hand, if you have always had a very honest and trusting relationship, you may ask yourself how can you not tell her, even if it upsets her.

Many people suffering from advanced dementia lack

the capacity to understand, and/or suffer short-term memory loss. You may have to repeat—and have her hear, process, and experience—a painful truth and emotional distress over and over.

Exploration

Almost 6 million people are diagnosed with Alzheimer's and related dementias in the U.S. today. And more than 55 million people worldwide have dementia, according to the World Health Organization.

So many caring relatives experience this deeply painful and personal question as a moral dilemma, as well as an emotional and practical challenge. The ethics focus here is on what is in the *best interest of the person diagnosed with dementia*. The prerequisite to acting is getting medical advice about the person's capacity to understand the information.

This is a rare situation when we may turn two forces that drive the ethics of virtually every decision we make— transparency and truth—on their head. One way of thinking about transparency is ensuring that we have the information important to understanding the potential consequences of our decision. Truth undergirds the ethics of all decisions. Both force us to ask whether there is a legitimate *reason* to prioritize transparency and truth over other considerations tugging at us, such as compassion, respect, autonomy, and dignity.

On the other hand, the person may feel unsafe or confused if they don't know what happened to the deceased person. Those who are able can use the information to grieve, to understand why the person close to them who has died is not communicating with them or visiting. But there is no obligation to give information to help the person make a choice because there are no choices to make at this stage. Consider whether there are alternative ways to make them feel safe, such as increasing your own visits, or working with medical staff for ideas.

Guilt has no place in ethics. It neither solves problems nor improves the quality of our decision making. In this case, it makes the decision about *us*, rather than about the relative living with dementia. Ethics are about decisions— not about labeling ourselves or others as "bad" or "good."

Some people believe that withholding the truth is wrong no matter what the circumstances or consequences. Lying almost always has consequences—even if not seemingly significant or immediate—and ethical decision making requires considering the consequences of our choices over time. But this is a very rare situation in which the consequences of truth may cause more harm. (I'm not arguing for lying if the person asks about the deceased relative.) And we should tread very carefully to assure that exceptional situations do not become excuses for, or a slippery slope to, compromising transparency and truth.

If you are making this heartbreaking decision in your own life, I am so sorry that you are going through this. Be compassionate with yourself as well. There is no one right answer, other than doing our best to reflect on the ethics of our decisions.

Would you be in favor of editing the genes of human embryos?

"Imagine a world where genetic engineering is determined mainly by individual free choice, with few government regulations and no pesky bioethics panels telling us what's permissible," postulates Walter Isaacson in his book *The Code Breaker*, about gene editing pioneer and Nobel laureate Jennifer A. Doudna. "You go into a fertility clinic and are given, as if at a genetic supermarket, a list of traits you can buy for your children." He concludes that most of us would choose to eliminate serious genetic diseases such as Huntington's or sickle cell. Personally, he tells us, he would eliminate blindness.

But it is easy to go careening down a slippery slope . . . what about editing genes to achieve a higher IQ? An individual's preferred height and build? If we leave use of this humanity-defining technology primarily to individual choice, Isaacson suggests that indeed "Without any gates or flags, we might all go barreling down at uncontrollable speed, taking society's diversity and the human genome along with us."

Gene editing allows genetic material in the cell to be added, removed, or changed. But there are two different kinds of gene editing, with very different ethical stakes. Editing the code of somatic, or nonreproductive cells, is not inheritable. For example, gene editing to cure cancer only affects the patient, not any future offspring. In contrast, so-called germline therapy, according to the National Human Genome Research Institute, "change[s] genes in reproductive cells (like sperm and eggs) . . . [which] would then be passed down from generation to generation."

Exploration

This question asks us to confront one of humanity's most critical challenges—as Jennifer A. Doudna says, "the general unease of humans taking control of their own evolution." I offer some key questions and my own (evolving) views to help you get your bearings—even if, like me, you don't fully understand the science.

First, think about who gets to decide when and how our genes can be edited. Among the potential list: governments, geneticists, doctors and hospitals, patients, parents, those planning to have children. All of the above have a role and responsibility *for individuals and for society.* Individuals should not have unregulated freedom to choose their children's genes. And regulators should not impede what Doudna calls "genetic surgery" to fix genetic defects in nonreproductive cells since the consequences cannot be passed down hereditarily from parent to children.

Next, how do we assure informed consent—that the

participants understand the *potential consequences* of gene editing. Science is complex and rapidly changing, and there is limited visibility of the clinical outcomes and side effects of gene editing in many cases. (As of this writing, editing embryos is generally not seen as ethically acceptable by the scientific community.)

Then we should ask how we prevent gene editing from being used as a weapon for bioterrorism. Certain types of gene editing can be done on a relatively low budget and by rogue individuals, unlike building a complex nuclear device.

Perhaps most importantly, gene editing should be seen as a potential opportunity for medical progress to improve human lives, not as an effort to fundamentally change who we are. Some people who have genetic diseases understandably wonder whether they would in fact want to edit their genes or the genes of their children, because they believe their illness is a fundamental part of who they are as a person. Isaacson introduces us to a young sickle cell patient who has suffered tremendously during his life but still isn't convinced he would choose to edit embryos to eliminate the disease.

My view is that we owe it to each other to consider whether eliminating the suffering of a life-threatening disease could offer patients greater health, autonomy, and respect and more *opportunity to make choices for themselves*. Scientists will have to tell us if and when it is safe, with proper oversight in place, to extend gene editing to human embryos. We all need to consider how we would explain to a child—our child—that we could have prevented their suffering but chose not to. Then there is the matter of equity. We will need to assure access to gene editing to cure diseases for all.

Losing out on an opportunity itself can be one of our biggest risks. Imagine losing the chance to cure cancer with gene editing (a nonheritable intervention). Now imagine the patient is you, or a loved one.

What is our ethical responsibility to get vaccinated?

I was taken aback when a friend's guitar teacher in London—a thirty-four-year-old accomplished teacher and performer—told her that he does not intend to get the Covid-19 vaccine. He has two young children who cannot yet be vaccinated and teaches in person at a middle school and secondary school. Usually very thoughtful, he seemed oblivious to the fact that the vaccine both protects him and diminishes transmission to colleagues, students, his family, and others. For him, it wasn't about religion, denying science, or politics—or even a particular fear or risk. He believed that the U.K. had already reached herd immunity (not true), and that others had done the heavy lifting on civic duty, so there was no need for him to make the effort to get a vaccine.

Contrast this with one fifty-seven-year-old friend of mine who faithfully gets all vaccinations (including the annual flu shot) but at the onset of the pandemic said she would rather quarantine than be a "guinea pig" with the Covid-19 vaccine. She changed her mind after seeing the lasting health and mental health consequences of the disease and of quarantine, not to mention how quickly the new variants can spread even with the best precautions.

As of April 2021, one in four Americans "would refuse a coronavirus vaccine outright if offered," according to an NPR/Marist survey. The CDC says the vaccines are highly effective at preventing severe illness and death resulting from a Covid-19 infection. All fifty states require mandatory vaccinations for diseases such as polio and measles with outstanding results. The World Health Organization and the Pan American Health Organization jointly declared that measles are officially eradicated in North and South America in 2016.

Exploration

Vaccine hesitancy is front and center with Covid-19, reinforcing the question of whether vaccines should be mandatory. The ethics start with science.

The choice is not simply whether to get vaccinated. It's a choice about what combination of steps we will take, and sacrifices we will make, to keep ourselves and others safe. This is even more true with the surge of new variants of the virus. At a minimum, those refusing vaccination must take every possible safety precaution, including wearing masks, social distancing, apprising others near them of their unvaccinated status, and getting tested frequently, while those who have been vaccinated may live, work, and socialize much more freely. In my view, we have no more right to expose others to Covid-19 than we do to drive while drunk. We don't get to free ride on others' vaccinations.

(To be clear, I'm not addressing those with doctor-excused medical reasons and sincerely held religious beliefs here; they might be exempt, as they were from mandatory measles vaccines decades ago.)

Vaccine hesitancy forces us to navigate principles that affect us all: health and safety (our own and that of others), truth (evidence-based science), and responsibility. To me, protecting human life in these unprecedented circumstances trumps some of the most important individual rights. I am particularly concerned about those who are at grave risk because their immune systems are compromised, children who cannot yet be vaccinated, and those who through no fault of their own don't have access to vaccines. We must also think of others who have no choice but to go to work and be exposed to the public.

Companies, schools and universities, and organizations have a duty to protect employees, customers, and the public. Everyone who enters a workplace should be required to prove vaccination—or provide a recent negative test, or demonstrate immunity from recent recovery from Covid-19. And with the rise of new variants, both vaccinations and masks (and even testing) might be necessary. Employees who refuse vaccines and are able to work remotely might need to continue to do so. Some may lose their jobs. French president Emmanuel Macron has declared proof of vaccination, or a very recent negative Covid-19 test, a prerequisite to entering cafés, restaurants, concert venues, and other public places.

Requiring transparency about one's vaccination status

is the only way to allow others to make informed decisions about whether they want to be in contact with an individual or enter an enclosed space. It's a minor compromise on privacy considering that we are each called to make potentially life-threatening choices as we work, socialize, and travel—and given that the carrot approach (access for those who are vaccinated to workplace gyms or free food) isn't working well enough to achieve herd immunity.

We all can fight for truth, calling on social media companies and the media not to disseminate false information about vaccines.

Intention is clear: the consequences of failing to vaccinate are widely known, so those declining vaccines are making a deliberate choice (even if few people consciously intend to harm others or get sick themselves).

We can encourage those who are hesitant to vaccinate to consider how they would feel if they caused someone else's illness or death. Think of the drunk driving videos used to educate high school students. We don't get to opt out of being responsible to others—whether we vaccinate or not and whatever our intentions may be.

Would you want artificial intelligence to contribute to diagnosing your medical condition?

An American friend of mine living in Paris made an appointment for a mammogram at the American Hospital of Paris. She emerged very excited, not just with the usual relief of a negative test, but with additional confidence: her radiologist had deployed artificial intelligence in analyzing the images, to be more efficient and effective. I was curious. For years I have had the privilege of serving on the board of governors of the American Hospital of Paris, as well as the hospital's ethics committee and patient care committee. When I checked the update to the hospital's website, I learned that the imaging department offers medical imaging "assisted by artificial intelligence . . . artificial intelligence (AI) does not replace the radiologist. It helps the radiologist to be more efficient and make a diagnosis more quickly. We have AI tools for segmenting brain structures, and detecting pulmonary nodules and breast microcalcifications."

Algorithms can detect patterns in images, work in

seconds, and are inexpensively reproduced. They don't get sick or tired. They do require accurate and representative data to train for accuracy, but they continually improve as more data is added. That said, they don't have much bedside manner (yet), and they cannot understand what it's like to be human (yet).

According to the American Medical Association, an AI program "can now diagnose skin cancer more accurately than a board-certified dermatologist . . . faster and more efficiently." In addition to diagnosis, *Harvard Business Review* reported a wide variety of promising medical applications, including robot-assisted surgery and dosage error reduction.

Exploration

It is imperative that ethics do not become a barrier to innovation; that is even more true when human health is at stake. Put yourself in the shoes of the person lucky enough to receive a cancer diagnosis from a machine much earlier than a human doctor could detect it, resulting in minor treatment with a positive outcome rather than a torturous treatment or worse. And consider the systemic benefits. An analysis by consultancy Accenture found that "key clinical health AI applications can potentially create $150 billion in annual savings for the US healthcare economy by 2026."

First, AI is a supplement to, not a replacement for, human oversight. It should be used in combination with human medical expertise and proper clinical care—a blended solution. Another critical concern is the potential impact of limited or skewed data used to train AI for diagnostic accuracy (for example, training data that is racially skewed or disproportionately represents a particular age group). But missing an opportunity to maximize diagnostic insights, save costs, greatly increase speed of results, and potentially save lives could be the greatest risk of all.

Then consider other concerns for patients and for society, particularly transparency, privacy, and inequality.

Medical ethics experts tell me that consent forms do not generally specify when AI is being used. This is another instance in which informed consent is not fully informed. I would argue that medical providers should be obligated to tell you whether they use AI in diagnostics, both to obtain consent to the use and to be sure you're not missing an important health care benefit.

And with so many global health matters, inequality is a major ethics challenge.

Google and its sister company Verily are testing an AI system in India that they developed to diagnose diabetic retinopathy, a condition that can lead to blindness if untreated. The Google project is part of a widespread effort to deploy systems that can automatically detect signs of illness where few eye doctors are available. (According to the International Council of Ophthalmology, there are only eleven eye doctors in India for every 1 million people.)

AI can be a force multiplier to spread good (or ill) faster than ever before. Your individual doctor and the medical institution are just as responsible for the use and confidentiality of AI as they are for using a scalpel or a prescription pad. Experts claim that artificial intelligence will be applicable to a vast array of medical fields, from diagnosing breast cancer, to predicting osteoarthritis years before there are symptoms, to recognizing rare diseases with facial recognition technology. We should ensure not only safety, but also access for all who wish to benefit from it.

Should vaping be banned?

Banana Ice. Unicorn Puke. Sweet Tart. "Every flavor Skittle compressed into one." Those are some of the flavors I found in 2015 when first researching e-cigarettes, battery-powered devices that look like USB drives, which deliver nicotine through a flavored liquid that is then heated and vaporized. E-cigarettes and other electronic nicotine delivery systems, or ENDS—vapes, vape pens, hookah pens, e-pipes—contain nicotine and other ingredients that are harmful to our health. The most popular e-cigarette in the U.S. is JUUL.

In 2016, it became illegal to sell e-cigarettes and electronic nicotine delivery systems to people under eighteen. In 2019, Congress raised the federal legal age to twenty-one.

Kevin Burns, the CEO of Juul Labs, urged viewers on *CBS This Morning* not to start vaping if they weren't already smokers. "Don't start using nicotine if you don't have a preexisting relationship with nicotine . . . You're not our target consumer."

On October 12, 2021, the FDA, for the first time, authorized the sale of a specific brand of e-cigarettes in the U.S.

The agency explained that based on available data, "the authorized products' aerosols are significantly less toxic" than cigarettes. The FDA stated that it would continue to monitor the marketing of e-cigarettes and take further action "if credible evidence emerges of significant use by individuals who did not previously use a tobacco product, including youth."

Exploration

This is an area where science, health, and medicine must rule the ethics. Remember that ethics may apply differently to youth and adults.

I strongly agree with the ban on purchasing e-cigarettes under twenty-one—not least because we don't have the information we need to trust the safety of the product. The jury is also still out on a range of safety and addiction issues, in the eyes of Dr. Norman E. Sharpless, the director of the National Cancer Institute. As Johns Hopkins Medicine reports, even the secondhand vapor from e-cigarettes has chemicals that can be harmful to children. There is also a concern that vaping will lead youths to escalate to real cigarettes.

The case for vaping may be more compelling for adults. Some adults see vaping as a healthier alternative for a long-standing cigarette addiction.

Companies and regulators owe the public transparency (clear statements of the risks *and the unknowns* in plain language like SMOKING KILLS on cigarette packages) and bans on manipulative advertising. (The five major U.S. smokeless tobacco companies spent $576.1 million on advertising and promotion in the U.S. in 2019, according to the Federal Trade Commission cigarette report.) Early studies suggest that vaping in order to quit smoking may lead to doing both interchangeably. Quitting smoking is incredibly difficult. But there are medically approved alternatives to vaping that can help smokers, from medications to nicotine patches to lozenges and gums.

These products engage a host of drivers in the spread of unwanted behavior: peer pressure, impunity, failed compliance (USB-size nicotine discs are extremely easy to hide), falsity (misleading advertising and social media), endorsements from celebrities, and greed as tobacco companies look for alternative revenue as smoking declines. All increase the popularity of vaping and illicit use by those underage and could renormalize and raise rates of smoking—which have been in decline for years—in the view of the American Heart Association.

We don't have enough information or studies on the long-term impact of vaping yet. Until we do, I believe it makes sense ethically to maintain laws prohibiting sale to minors and discourage the marketing and use of such products, but leave the choice to consenting adults and their medical advisors. It's easy to think that our ethical responsibility ends once a law is enacted. But as the FDA rightly emphasized, laws require monitoring, particularly as science reveals new information (as we learned from regulations on cigarette smoking, where we did far too little for far too long and adult behavior was copied by children and teens). Vaping is a reminder that we need other stakeholders such as companies and regulators to do their part to support our choices.

How do you decide if you should donate a kidney to a close friend or relative?

Aclose relative—your child or sister—is experiencing kidney failure. They need a transplant to save their life. After getting tested and examined, doctors determine you are a match and that the surgery would be safe for both of you.

There are 100,000 patients on the kidney transplant list. According to the Donor Care Network, there are 5,000 living donors in the U.S. every year who donate a kidney. In 2020, only 21,000 donor organs (from living and deceased donors) were available for transplant.

Exploration

This is a highly personal and emotional question that hinges on the individual facts and your personal perspective.

You have the power to save a life. But this is one time when you don't have a responsibility to use it. Nor are you responsible for the health consequences of the recipient. You do not owe anyone one of your organs. Similarly, the recipient can refuse a donation—for any number of reasons, not the least of which is concern over the donor's health or family relationships if a family member is involved.

The threshold question we have to answer before anything else is medical, not ethical: Get all the information you can get about *your specific situation*, from experts. Ask whether there is anything you don't know that you should. You might also confirm whether, in your situation, patients who receive an organ from a living donor have a higher success rate than those who receive an organ from someone who had died.

The ability to save another person's life is a gift beyond words. But it does require that one think about the short-, medium-, and long-term consequences. Don't expect that exercising such generosity and compassion will change how the other person feels about you, or how willing they would be to help at a future time should you or your loved one be in need. Also, catapult yourself into the future: imagine if one of your children or grandchildren needs a kidney, and you no longer have the ability to donate one. Should you consider the recipient's life expectancy—an eighty-eight-year-old grandparent versus your fifty-year-old brother? Think about how close you are to your relative. Ask whether other donors are available.

Consider putting this question on a spectrum of potential family obligations, such as whether we owe family members medical care if they cannot afford it. Do family members have to earn our financial and emotional support, or do you feel they have some sort of inherent right based on the family ties? Organ donation is at the extreme end of the spectrum—again, in my view we do not owe anyone the donation of a kidney.

This question forces us to broaden the lens: it reminds us that the personal ethical questions we face and the broader societal questions are interlinked. Family and friend donation decisions have a domino effect on a growing societal need for organs for transplant.

Donating an organ to a friend or relative can be compassionate, courageous, and generous. But there are many valid reasons not to donate, depending on your circumstances, and theirs. There is no one right answer. Whatever the ethics analysis, the decision will be fraught with emotion. What we can do is to show compassion to anyone in a position to consider donating, or needing, an organ.

Conclusion:
We Can All Do Ethics

When I set out to write this book, the list of potential questions seemed unlimited. Just as I settled on a selection, new questions popped up on the morning news, at the supermarket, in my class at Stanford, on family Zoom calls, and beyond—whether concerns arising out of the Covid-19 pandemic, new state voting restrictions, children's mental health, or the killing of George Floyd and the subsequent murder trial and verdict.

With the help of wise advisors, I chose questions across a broad spectrum. My goal: to offer an ethics arena in which you, the reader, could grapple with a mix of familiar and "never heard of" dilemmas. But the book's learning applies to every question I could have selected. I thank you for joining the conversation, debating the challenges that I pose and their effects on you individually, on family and friends, on work, on society, on our hearts and minds, on technology and tradition, on today's politics and priorities, and on tomorrow's problems and promise. I thank you for probing areas that may initially have seemed outside your personal knowledge or comfort zone, or don't seem that relevant to your life.

Now, your journey continues. The book is an invitation to see ethics in every choice we make. Not as a burden, but as a helpful habit, and a way of exercising our personal power. I hope you feel better equipped to tackle the ethical challenges you will inevitably face, as well as to express and debate your views, and to accept that we all live with uncertainty, and even error. Ethics do not require physical fitness, a hefty bank account, a certain level of education, or a title. It's a way of thinking we can all participate in. And I believe that our progress as a society is dependent on everyone embracing ethics. No political or corporate leader, institution, regulator, or citizen can do it alone. As much as we need stronger systems and institutional change, our systems start with, and must be held accountable to, individuals.

I hope you have come to see ethics as stories . . . stories that show that each of us has the power . . . and responsibility . . . to influence one another for the better. We are never the only characters in our stories. The upside: decision by decision we can craft a better story for ourselves and all whose lives we are privileged to touch.

Occasionally there is a single right answer—eradicate racism, counter disinformation on the internet, expose and oppose sexual misconduct. More often, there are many possible outcomes or narratives. Our task is to courageously wade through the gray areas in life—to seek opportunity and mitigate risk.

Ethics happen in real time . . . with no guarantees. We cannot control the actions or behaviors of others. We cannot custom design the world as we wish it were. Our power comes not from an unrealistic quest for control but rather from navigating the real world in which we often lack control. From building on truth, not wishful thinking. The world does not owe us to be the way we want it to be. And just because we believe it to be a particular way will not make it so.

Ethics are *proactive*. All manner of unfortunate outcomes, from unconscious bias to lack of compassion, can be traced back to our neutrality or passivity.

Ethics are *inclusive*. Questions that may seem far from our everyday concerns in fact touch us more directly than we might have imagined. Dilemmas that may seem separate and distinct often have a shared foundation. There is common ground among virtually every ethical conundrum in the book, as well as those you will face in your own life.

We're only as ethical as our last decision. Labels or categories—even "ethical" or "unethical"—are shortcuts, not thoughtful ethics. They create divisiveness and polarization rather than informed, compassionate connection.

When in doubt, we all should ask what our decision looks like from the point of view of the person most adversely affected. Then imagine that person is us or a loved one.

Before we judge, we all should query whether we really know as much as we think we know—where might assumptions (shortcuts, gut feelings, unverified social media posts, casual or even lazy thinking) be driving (or justifying) our choices?

We can be ethically resilient when we tell the truth, take

responsibility, and make a concrete plan to ensure that any unwanted behavior isn't repeated.

As you share stories, always ask if it's your story to tell. Look for every opportunity to shout out someone else's success—and pass up every chance to call out a weakness or error. Then ask if it's a story you must tell.

We must always keep human beings and humanity front and center. We should require our leaders to prioritize ethical decision making and to listen to those they have responsibility to lead—rather than attempting to dictate society's ethics or, worse, give themselves a pass.

Trust yourself. Enjoy your ethics. As mythologist and author Joseph Campbell said, "The privilege of a lifetime is being who you are." Ethics are a path for each of us becoming who we are. I believe that ethics are the greatest connector—binding us to one another and to our shared humanity.

The Six Forces
Driving Ethics

Throughout this book, you will have seen references to six forces that I believe influence the ethics of every choice we make. You will quickly come to recognize these forces in the questions and explorations in the book (whether or not explicitly stated) and in your own life. Here is a quick primer.

Banish the binary: Ethics are not a "yes or no" or "do it or don't do it" choice. Some ethics failures are indeed straight-up unacceptable: racism, sexual misconduct, and disregarding science-based evidence about Covid-19. But most questions we face require navigating a gray zone. Rather than just labeling options as "right or wrong" or "ethical or unethical," banishing the binary prompts us to ask, *When and under what circumstances should we proceed?* You will have seen throughout the book an emphasis on *seizing opportunity* and *mitigating risk* rather than choosing sides.

Scattered power: Today, power is no longer concentrated only in the hands of a few; it's more scattered than ever.

Think of the power you have with your cell phone—to contribute to a political campaign or tutor a child across the country . . . or incite violence. The challenge today is to reconnect power to ethical responsibility . . . and to recognize that we each have a role: no president or corporate behemoth can deliver, or repair, moral decline alone. Every choice matters. Every choice is an opportunity to reconnect our power to our ethics—whether wearing a mask or speaking up against a racist remark.

Contagion: Ethics are contagious—for good or for ill. But we often focus so much on the unwanted behavior (fraud, social media data privacy, not wearing masks) that we ignore the factors that drove the *spreading* of the behavior—leaving them to fester and spur further trouble. While we know fake news can distort our choices, we have not adequately addressed the contagion drivers such as the misuse of the internet, lack of user-friendly transparency, ineffective regulation, corporate greed, and extremism, to name a few. The hopeful news: once we identify and dismantle these drivers, and deploy them for good, our choices can have a lasting impact. We will learn from mistakes and stop seeing the same headlines over and over again in the news.

Pillars of ethics: Transparency and (un)informed consent are two long-standing pillars of ethical decision making. They depend on understanding what's at stake in our decisions (short- and longer-term) but are crumbling in today's complex, technological world. Think of getting your tonsils removed: you understand the benefits and risks well enough, and you're clear about the procedure and recovery steps like an ice cream diet for a few days. Now think of artificial intelligence diagnosing skin cancer. Or how you feel when you click "I agree" on social media terms of service. But we can learn to recalibrate what we mean by transparency and informed consent—particularly the information and commitment to our understanding prior to soliciting consent that we expect of companies and governments.

Blurred boundaries: Blurred boundaries are everywhere today: human and machine, human and animal, and increasingly work and home. We are in uncharted, sometimes uncomfortable, territory as we think about the role of robots in society (receptionists, caring for the elderly, nannies, driverless cars), looking to animals for medical treatment (growing organs in pigs for human transplant), and beyond. We must keep humanity front and center and assure that humans take responsibility for the blur . . . and for reclarifying boundaries.

Compromised truth: Ethics hinge on truth. There is no such thing as post-truth or alternatively factual ethics. Today, truth is under threat in unprecedented ways from denial of science and other factual information to distrust of experts to algorithmic distortion of our news feeds and social media bubbles shielding us from diverse views. This compromised truth removes our choices from reality. But as I tell my students, we can do ethics in a world of wishful thinking or cherry-picked la-la land all we want, but reality—truth—will come back to bite. It is very real for us, and for others, in terms of the consequences of our choices. Compromised truth topples social relationships and institutions (including democracy) and threatens ethics. And its impact lasts: today's skewed truth becomes tomorrow's distorted memory and history.

Acknowledgments

The Little Book of Big Ethical Questions started with a meeting I was fortunate to have with Simon & Schuster CEO Jonathan Karp; executive editor Stephanie Frerich; and my agent, Kathy Robbins, about my first book, *The Power of Ethics*. Jon's idea for a series of conversation starters, and the question-and-answer format, fit so perfectly with my own mission of democratizing ethics. I couldn't be more grateful to write this book with Simon & Schuster, and to have a second opportunity to work with Stephanie.

The work continued over several years, with many varied conversations. I have cherished every exchange—whether with my black-cab driver in London, a podcast interviewer, fellow passengers disembarking from a canceled flight, at a dinner with friends, in line for a coffee or even a Covid-19 vaccination, in class with students, or on family FaceTime calls. I learned so much from conversations that extraordinary writers recorded in their own works of nonfiction and fiction, in the media, and on social media—too many to name.

As one of my wise advisors noted, writing a book takes a village. It was a privilege to work with the Simon & Schuster team: associate editor Emily Simonson was professional, efficient, and so thoughtful in her commentary; Fred Chase, an extraordinary copy editor, improved every page; cover designer Ryan Raphael and art director Alison Forner created the perfect jacket design (including one that continued the visuals seamlessly from their design for *The Power of Ethics*); Sara Kitchen (production editor); Beth Maglione (production manager); Paul Dippolito (interior designer); Jordan Koluch (proofreader); and Amanda Mulholland (managing editor) turned these thoughts into an accessible visual experience. And my thanks to publicist Cat Boyd and marketer Leila Siddiqui for crafting the message.

I am grateful to Roger Scholl for bringing his decades of literary expertise and immense editing talent to the project. He was very patient with my insistence that things are not as obvious or settled as they may first appear—and with my struggle to stay within our set word count.

As I said in *The Power of Ethics*, meeting my agent, Kathy Robbins, was one of life's great moments. This project never would have come to life without her wisdom, editorial insights, and support. It was such a pleasure as well to work with her Robbins Office colleagues Janet Oshiro and Alexandra Sugarman, who assured that all ran smoothly.

Lisa Sweetingham provided such valuable perspective and commentary just when I needed it most. I so value her thoughtfulness, writing talent, and research rigor.

For the past several years, I have had the pleasure of teaching and working with many meticulous students, research assistants, and teaching assistants. I am especially grateful for the open-minded, committed, and effective contributions of Daria Lenz, Ariadne Nichol, Megan Olomu, and Carolina Sculti. Clint Akarmann's wise observations and Joseph Zabel's insightful commentary improved many of the questions.

My gratitude to my trusted colleague of many years, Anna Barberà i Aresté, whose efficacy and contributions have been essential to my nonprofit platform, The Ethics Incubator, and both books.

Finally, to my children, Luca, Olivia, Parker, Alexa, and Cristo, for believing in me, and my husband, Bernard. I learn from you every day with every question we face.

And my gratitude to you, the reader, for taking the time to read, explore, discuss, reflect, and challenge yourself and others.

Notes

INTRODUCTION: ETHICS FOR EVERYONE

3   *Impossible Burger*: "What are the ingredients in Impossible™ Burger?" Impossible Foods, accessed October 8, 2021, faq.impos siblefoods.com/hc/en-us/articles/360018937494-What-are-the-in gredients-in-Impossible-Burger-.

CHAPTER 1: FAMILY AND FRIENDS

18   *"Love thy neighbor":* Matthew 22:36–39, New Testament, *The Bible*, cs monitor.com/Commentary/A-Christian-Science-Perspective/2008 /0327/p18s02-hfcs.html.

18   *"The more we care":* Tenzin Gyatso (the fourteenth Dalai Lama), "Compassion and the Individual," *His Holiness the 14th Dalai Lama of Tibet*, accessed September 5, 2021, dalailama.com/messages /compassion-and-human-values/compassion.

21   *According to the U.S. Census Bureau*: Katherine Keisler-Starkey and Lisa N. Bunch, *Health Insurance Coverage in the United States: 2019*, United States Census Bureau, September 15, 2020, census.gov /library/publications/2020/demo/p60-271.html.

21   *the Census Bureau reports*: Ibid.

21   *National Health Service*: "How does universal health coverage work?" The Commonwealth Fund, commonwealthfund.org/international -health-policy-center/system-features/how-does-universal-health -coverage-work.

24   *widely read*: Mary McNamara, "The Diary of Anne Frank," *Los Ange-les Times*, April 10, 2010, latimes.com/archives/la-xpm-2010-apr-10 -la-et-frank-review10-2010apr10-story.html.

25   *doctor-patient confidentiality*: Kristin E. Schleiter, JD, "When Patient-Physician Confidentiality Conflicts with the Law," *AMA Journal of Ethics* 11, no. 2 (February 2009): 146–48, journalofethics.ama-assn

.org/article/when-patient-physician-confidentiality-conflicts-law
/2009-02.

30 *adult children prevailed in court*: Palko Karasz, "French Rock Star's
Instagram Defeats His Widow in Inheritance Battle," *New York Times*,
May 29, 2019, nytimes.com/2019/05/29/world/europe/johnny-hally
day-instagram-will.html.

31 *Napoleonic Code*: *Encyclopaedia Britannica Online*, s.v. "Napoleonic
Code," accessed December 12, 2021, britannica.com/topic/Napo
leonic-Code.

31 *ethical wills*: Deborah Quilter, "The Ethical Will: Life Is About More
than Your Possessions," Next Avenue, April 11, 2019, nextavenue.org
/ethical-will; Wikipedia, s.v. "Ethical will," accessed September 22,
2021, en.wikipedia.org/wiki/Ethical_will.

33 *23andMe*: "How it works," 23andMe, accessed September 22, 2021,
23andme.com/en-gb/howitworks.

33 *more than 26 million*: Antonio Regalado, "Is the consumer genetics
fad over?" *MIT Technology Review*, January 23, 2020, technologyre
view.com/2020/01/23/276092/is-the-consumer-genetics-fad-over.

34 *23andMe warns on its website*: "Terms of Service," 23andMe, last
modified September 30, 2019, 23andme.com/about/tos.

35 *The American Society of Human Genetics*: Deborah Levenson, "American society of human genetics updates guidance on genetic testing
in children," *American Journal of Medical Ethics* 167, no. 10 (October
2015): viii–ix, onlinelibrary.wiley.com/doi/full/10.1002/ajmg.a.37357.

46 *.08 g/dL or higher*: "Drunk Driving," National Highway Traffic Safety
Administration, United States Department of Transportation, accessed September 22, 2021, nhtsa.gov/risky-driving/drunk driving.

46 *three drinks*: "Blood Alcohol Level Chart: Are You Too Drunk to Legally Drive?" DrivingLaws, accessed September 22, 2021, dui.driving
laws.org/drink-table.php.

47 *died in a drunk-driving accident*: "Drunk Driving," National Highway
Traffic Safety Administration, accessed September 22, 2021, nhtsa
.gov/risky-driving/drunk-driving.

47 *28 percent of all fatal car accidents*: "Traffic Safety Facts 2019," U.S.
Department of Transportation National Highway Traffic Safety Administration, August 2021, https://crashstats.nhtsa.dot.gov/Api/Pub
lic/ViewPublication/813141.

51 *The* Oxford Advanced Learner's Dictionary *defines cheating*: *Oxford
Advanced Learner's Dictionary*, s.v. "cheat (n.)," oxfordlearnersdictio
naries.com/definition/english/cheat_2.

51 *something for sale*: Michael Sandel, "Are There Things Money Shouldn't Be Able to Buy?" Oxford Union, video, May 10, 2015, you tube.com/watch?v=zMg9Gjz8PKs.

52 *Sandel makes a critical point*: Ibid.

56 *graduation speech*: "Adm. McRaven Urges Graduates to Find Courage to Change the World," UT News, May 16, 2014, news.utexas.edu /2014/05/16/mcraven-urges-graduates-to-find-courage-to-change -the-world.

57 *"will encourage you to do another task"*: Admiral William H. McRaven, *Make Your Bed: Little Things That Can Change Your Life . . . and Maybe the World* (New York: Grand Central Publishing, 2017).

57 *If you want to change*: Ibid., University of Texas's commencement speech to be found at the back of the book.

CHAPTER 2: POLITICS, COMMUNITY, AND CULTURE

63 *Hurricane Katrina*: History.com Editors, "Hurricane Katrina," History .com, August 31, 2021, accessed December 12, 2021, history.com/top ics/natural-disasters-and-environment/hurricane-katrina.

63 *There was almost no food*: German Lopez, "Hurricane Katrina, in 7 essential facts," *Vox*, August 28, 2015, vox.com/2015/8/23/9191907 /hurricane-katrina.

64 *one of the costliest hurricanes*: Eric S. Blake and Ethan J. Gibney, *The Deadliest, Costliest, and Most Intense United States Tropical Cyclones from 1851 to 2010 (And Other Frequently Requested Hurricane Facts)*, NOAA Technical Memorandum NWS NHC-6, August 2011, nhc.noaa.gov/pdf/nws-nhc-6.pdf.

64 *"looters floated"*: "Chaotic Conditions in New Orleans," CBS News, August 30, 2005, cbsnews.com/news/chaotic-conditions-in-new-or leans.

64 *Police responses were inconsistent*: Sabrina Shankman et al., "After Katrina, New Orleans Cops Were Told They Could Shoot Looters," ProPublica, July 24, 2012, propublica.org/article/nopd-order-to-shoot -looters-hurricane-katrina. See also Jeff Brady, "New Orleans Housing Prisoners in Bus Station," NPR, September 9, 2005, npr.org/tem plates/story/story.php?storyId=4838671.

70 *Compulsory or mandatory voting*: "What Is Compulsory Voting?" FindLaw, last modified March 16, 2020, findlaw.com/voting/how-u -s--elections-work/what-is-compulsory-voting-.html.

70 *More than twenty countries have mandatory voting requirements*:

Laura Santhanam, "22 countries where voting is mandatory," PBS, November 3, 2014, pbs.org/newshour/politics/22-countries-voting-mandatory.

70 *Australia passed mandatory voting*: Nina Jaffe-Geffner, "The Pros and Cons of Requiring Citizens to Vote," FairVote, October 23, 2015, fairvote.org/the_pros_and_cons_of_requiring_citizens_to_vote. See also "Prime Facts: Elections and voting in Australia," Australian Prime Ministers Centre, Museum of Australian Democracy, accessed December 1, 2021, static.moadoph.gov.au/ophgovau/media/images/apmc/docs/62-Elections.pdf.

70 *Over 91 percent*: "Turnout," *Australia Electoral Commission Annual Report 2018–19*, Australian Government Transparency Portal, accessed December 1, 2021, transparency.gov.au/annual-reports/Australian-electoral-commission/reporting-year/2018-2019-11.

70 *In the 2016 presidential election*: Gregory Wallace, "Voter turnout at 20-year low in 2016," CNN, last modified November 30, 2016, cnn.com/2016/11/11/politics/popular-vote-turnout-2016/index.html.

70 *In 2020*: Domenico Montanaro, "President-Elect Joe Biden Hits 80 Million Votes in Year of Record Turnout," NPR, November 25, 2020, npr.org/2020/11/25/937248659/president-elect-biden-hits-80-million-votes-in-year-of-record-turnout; United States Census Bureau, "2020 Presidential Election Voting and Registration Tables Now Available," news release no. CB21-TPS.49, April 29, 2021, census.gov/newsroom/press-releases/2021/2020-presidential-election-voting-and-registration-tables-now-available.html.

70 *Georgia passed a slew of laws*: Nick Corasaniti and Reid J. Epstein, "What Georgia's Voting Law Really Does," *New York Times*, April 2, 2021, nytimes.com/2021/04/02/us/politics/georgia-voting-law-annotated.html; Election Integrity Act of 2021, Georgia State Senate Bill 202 (2021), legiscan.com/GA/text/SB202/id/2348602/Georgia-2021-SB202-Enrolled.pdf.

71 *Florida and Texas*: Corasaniti and Epstein, "What Georgia's Voting Law Really Does."

71 *Advocates of mandatory voting*: Melissa De Witte, "Stanford political scientist makes the case for mandatory voting," Stanford News, November 30, 2018, news.stanford.edu/2018/11/30/case-mandatory-voting.

74 *580,000 people experienced homelessness*: U.S. Department of Housing and Urban Development, *The 2020 Annual Homeless As-*

sessment Report (AHAR) to Congress, January 2021, huduser.gov /portal/sites/default/files/pdf/2020-AHAR-Part-1.pdf.

75 *2021 study in high-income countries*: Stefan Gutwinski et al., "The prevalence of mental disorders among homeless people in high-income countries: An updated systematic review and meta-regression analysis," *PLoS Medicine* 18, no. 8 (August 2021), journals .plos.org/plosmedicine/article?id=10.1371/journal.pmed.1003750.

77 *Benin Bronzes*: Barnaby Phillips, "No Revolvers, Gentlemen, No Revolvers," chap. 4 in *Loot: Britain and the Benin Bronzes* (London: Oneworld Publications, 2021). See also Alex Marshall, "This Art Was Looted 123 Years Ago; Will It Ever Be Returned?" *New York Times*, January 23, 2020, nytimes.com/2020/01/23/arts/design/benin-bronzes.html.

77 *twenty-six of the stolen artifacts*: Aaron Ross and Marine Pennetier, "France returns 26 artworks to Benin as report urges restitution," Reuters, November 23, 2018, reuters.com/article/us-africa-france-art -idUSKCN1NS1GH.

78 *Netherlands announced*: "Government: Redressing an injustice by returning cultural heritage objects to their country of origin," Government of the Netherlands, January 29, 2021, government.nl /latest/news/2021/01/29/government-redressing-an-injustice-by -returning-cultural-heritage-objects-to-their-country-of-origin.

78 *Metropolitan Museum of Art has had to reassess*: Colin Moynihan, "Met Museum to Return Prize Artifact Because It Was Stolen," *New York Times*, February 15, 2019, nytimes.com/2019/02/15/arts/design /met-museum-stolen-coffin.html.

81 Leaving Neverland: Anastasia Tsioulcas, "Michael Jackson: A Quarter-Century of Sexual Abuse Allegations," NPR, March 5, 2019, npr.org /2019/03/05/699995484/michael-jackson-a-quarter-century-of -sexual-abuse-allegations.

81 Thriller: Tom Huddleston Jr., "Michael Jackson's iconic 'Thriller' is 36 today—and it's still the world's best-selling album," CNBC, November 30, 2018, cnbc.com/2018/11/30/michael-jacksons-thriller-anniver sary-still-all-time-best-seller.html. See also "Gold & Platinum," Recording Industry Association of America, RIAA.com/gold-platinum /?tab_active=top_tallies&ttt=TIA#search_section.

81 *Michael Jackson was never convicted*: Zack O'Malley Greenburg, "Michael Jackson's Earnings: $825 Million in 2016," *Forbes*, October 14, 2016, forbes.com/sites/zackomalleygreenburg/2016/10/14 /michael-jacksons-earnings-825-million-in-2016/?sh=2ab87f393d72.

See also Ben Sisario, "What We Know About Michael Jackson's History of Sexual Abuse Accusations," *New York Times*, January 31, 2019, ny times.com/2019/01/31/arts/music/michael-jackson-timeline-sexual -abuse-accusations.html.

81   *twenty-three years in prison*: Jan Ransom, "Harvey Weinstein's Stunning Downfall: 23 Years in Prison," *New York Times*, last modified June 15, 2021, nytimes.com/2020/03/11/nyregion/harvey-weinstein -sentencing.html.

81   *nine counts*: Troy Closson, "R. Kelly Is Convicted of All Counts After Decades of Accusations of Abuse," *New York Times*, September 27, 2021, nytimes.com/2021/09/27/nyregion/r-kelly-verdict-racketeering -sex-trafficking.html.

84   *the youngest U.S. president*: Associated Press, "France's Emmanuel Macron joins Trudeau in ranks of youngest world leaders," CBC News, May 8, 2017, cbc.ca/news/world/france-macron-trudeau-youngest -world-leaders-1.4105670.

84   *U.S. Presidential candidates must be*: "Requirements for the President of the United States," Library of Congress, loc.gov/classroom -materials/elections/presidential-election-process/requirements-for -the-president-of-the-united-states.

84   *Neither the Democratic frontrunners nor President Trump*: Dan Diamond, "Democratic candidates, Trump agree: Their medical records are none of your business," *Politico*, February 19, 2020, politico.com /news/2020/02/19/2020-democrats-medical-histories-116039.

84   *some medical documents and letters*: Susan Milligan, "Biden Releases Medical Records," *U.S. News & World Report*, December 17, 2019, usnews.com/news/elections/articles/2019-12-17/Biden-releases -medical-records.

85   *passed away at eighty-seven*: Linda Greenhouse, "Ruth Bader Ginsburg, Supreme Court's Feminist Icon, Is Dead at 87," *New York Times*, September 18, 2020, nytimes.com/2020/09/18/us/ruth-bader-gins burg-dead.html.

86   *companies are permitted*: Age Discrimination in Employment Act of 1967, 29 U.S.C. § 621 (2011), eeoc.gov/statutes/age-discrimination -employment-act-1967.

86   *commercial airline pilots*: Federal Aviation Administration, *Fair Treatment of Experienced Pilots Act (The Age 65 Law) Information, Questions and Answers*, May 9, 2019, faa.gov/other_visit/aviation_industry /airline_operators/airline_safety/info/all_infos/media/age65_qa.pdf.

86   *military personnel*: Retirement for Age, 10 U.S.C. § 63 (2010), govinfo

.gov/content/pkg/USCODE-2010-title10/html/USCODE-2010-title10
-subtitleA-partII-chap63.htm.

88 *Crucial runoff elections*: Matthew Impelli, "Georgia Senate Runoffs
    Finish as Most Expensive in History, At Least 171 Million More Than
    Any Other," *Newsweek*, January 6, 2021. See also Emma Green,
    "Georgia's Billion-Dollar Bonfire," *The Atlantic*, January 5, 2021, the
    atlantic.com/politics/archive/2021/01/money-spent-georgia-senate
    -runoffs/617545.

88 *According to FiveThirtyEight*: Chris Zubak-Skees, Nathaniel Rakich,
    and Julia Wolfe, "Where Are Georgia's Senate Candidates Getting All
    That Cash From?" FiveThirtyEight, December 9, 2020, fivethirtyeight
    .com/features/where-are-georgias-senate-candidates-getting-all
    -that-cash-from.

89 *And 92 percent*: Ibid.

89 *Current law often permits*: "State Limits on Contributions to Candi-
    dates, 2021–2022 Election Cycle, National Conference of State Legis-
    latures," National Conference of State Legislatures, last modified June
    2021, ncsl.org/Portals/1/Documents/Elections/Contribution_Limits
    _to_Candidates_2020_2021.pdf.

90 *"stand your ground"*: FindLaw Staff, "States That Have Stand Your
    Ground Laws," FindLaw, last modified June 2, 2020, findlaw.com
    /criminal/criminal-law-basics/states-that-have-stand-your-ground
    -laws.html.

90 Citizens United: Matt Bai, "How Much Has Citizens United Changed
    the Political Game?" *New York Times*, July 17, 2012, nytimes.com/2012
    /07/22/magazine/how-much-has-citizens-united-changed-the-polit
    ical-game.html; "Citizens United v. FEC," U.S. Federal Election Com-
    mission, fec.gov/legal-resources/court-cases/citizens-united-v-fec.

90 *"have no consciences, no beliefs"*: Citizens United v. FEC, 558 U.S.
    (2010), law.cornell.edu/supct/pdf/08-205P.ZX. See also "Citizens
    United v. FEC," FEC, fec.gov/legal-resources/court-cases/citizens
    -united-v-fec/, pp. 57, 81, 76.

91 *Justice Stevens believed*: Daniel Rothberg, "Retired Justice John
    Paul Stevens tells Congress 'money is not speech,'" *Los Angeles
    Times*, April 30, 2014, latimes.com/nation/politics/politicsnow/la-pn
    -supreme-court-stevens-congress-money-speech-20140430-story
    .html; *U.S. Senate Rules and Administration Committee Hearing on
    campaign finance law*, 113th Cong. 2 (2014) (statement of Justice
    John Paul Stevens [Ret.]), supremecourt.gov/publicinfo/speeches
    /JPSSpeech(DC)04-30-2014.pdf.

92 *In a recent case*: National Collegiate Athletic Association v. Alston, 594 U.S. (2021), supremecourt.gov/opinions/20pdf/20-512_gfbh.pdf.

92 *The Court disagreed*: Ibid.

92 *"massive business"*: Ibid.

93 *total revenues*: "Finances of Intercollegiate Athletics," NCAA, accessed November 30, 2021, ncaa.org/about/resources/research/fi nances-intercollegiate-athletics.

93 *$16 million*: Jo Craven McGinty, "March Madness Is a Moneymaker. Most Schools Still Operate in Red," *Wall Street Journal*, March 12, 2021, wsj.com/articles/march-madness-is-a-moneymaker-most-schools -still-operate-in-red-11615545002.

93 *fifty hours a week training*: Thomas Wright-Piersanti, "Change Comes to the N.C.A.A.," *New York Times*, June 22, 2021, nytimes.com /2021/06/22/briefing/ncaa-scotus-ruling.html.

93 *scholarships*: "A Guide to College Basketball Scholarships for High School Students," Next College Student Athlete, ncsasports.org /mens-basketball/scholarships.

94 *Athletes hoping to turn professional*: Zack Lowe, "Memo: NBA draft eligibility could shift by 2021," ESPN.com, June 15, 2018, espn.com /nba/story/_/id/23804458/memo-states-nba-draft-eligibility-shift-21.

94 *1.2 percent of men's basketball players*: NCAA, *Estimated Probability of Competing in College Athletics*, April 8, 2020, ncaaorg.s3.ama zonaws.com/research/pro_beyond/2019RES_ProbabilityBeyondHS FiguresMethod.pdf.

94 *Recent legal changes*: Meghan Roos, "26 States Now Allow College Athletes to Be Compensated for Image, Likeness," *Newsweek*, July 14, 2021, newsweek.com/26-states-now-allow-college-athletes -compensated-image-likeness-1609744.

95 *The NCAA announced*: Michelle Brutlag Hosick, "NCAA adopts interim name, image, and likeness policy," NCAA, June 30, 2021, ncaa .org/about/resources/media-center/news/ncaa-adopts-interim -name-image-and-likeness-policy.

95 *Justice Brett Kavanaugh*: National Collegiate Athletic Association v. Alston, 594 U.S. (2021).

96 *stop publishing six*: Bill Chappell, "Dr. Seuss Enterprises Will Shelve 6 Books, Citing 'Hurtful' Portrayals," NPR, March 2, 2021, npr.org/2021 /03/02/972777841/dr-seuss-enterprises-will-shelve-6-books-citing -hurtful-portrayals.

96 *Among the six were*: Ibid.

97   If I Ran the Zoo: Ibid.; Jenny Gross, "6 Dr. Seuss Books Will No Lon-
     ger Be Published Over Offensive Images," *New York Times*, March 2,
     2021, nytimes.com/2021/03/02/books/dr-seuss-mulberry-street.html.

98   *Roald Dahl reimagined*: Alexandra Alter and Elizabeth A. Har-
     ris, "Dr. Seuss Books Are Pulled and a 'Cancel Culture' Controver-
     sy Erupts," *New York Times*, last modified October 20, 2021, ny
     times.com/2021/03/04/books/dr-seuss-books.html. See also Kate
     Cantrell and David Burton, "From pygmies to puppets: what to do
     with Roald Dahl's enslaved Oompa-Loompas in modern adapta-
     tions?" The Conversation, September 15, 2021, theconversation.com
     /from-pygmies-to-puppets-what-to-do-with-Roald-Dahls-enslaved
     -oompa-loompas-in-modern-adaptations-166967.

98   *New Jersey state lawmakers*: Allison Pries, "Lawmakers want to
     expel Huckleberry Finn from N.J. schools," NJ.com, last modified
     March 23, 2019, nj.com/education/2019/03/lawmakers-want-to-ex
     pel-huckleberry-finn-from-nj-schools.html; Benedicte Page, "New
     Huckleberry Finn edition censors 'n-word,'" *The Guardian*, January 5,
     2011, theguardian.com/books/2011/jan/05/huckleberry-finn-edition
     -censors-n-word.

99   *"In a cultural landscape"*: Ross Douthat, "Do Liberals Care if Books
     Disappear?" *New York Times*, March 6, 2021, nytimes.com/2021/03
     /06/opinion/dr-seuss-books-liberalism.html.

100 *a sixty-nine-year-old Dutchman*: "Emile Ratelband, 69, told he can-
     not legally change his age," BBC News, December 3, 2018, bbc.com
     /news/world-europe-46425774.

100 *"all kinds of legal problems"*: Ibid.

103 *Sha'Carri Richardson*: Kevin Draper and Juliet Macur, "Sha'Carri Rich-
     ardson, a Track Sensation, Tests Positive for Marijuana," *New York
     Times*, last modified July 6, 2021, nytimes.com/2021/07/01/sports
     /olympics/shacarri-richardson-suspended-marijuana.html.

103 *4x100-meter relay*: Ibid.

103 *"I am human"*: Drew Weisholz, "Sha'Carri Richardson speaks out
     about failing drug test ahead of Olympics," *Today*, July 2, 2021, to
     day.com/news/today-show-exclusive-sha-carri-richardson-speaks
     -out-about-failing-t224363.

104 *"Pretty convinced"*: Nicholas Thompson (@nxthompson), "Pretty
     convinced that marijuana is not a 'performance enhancing' drug
     for a sprinter," Twitter, July 2, 2021, twitter.com/nxthompson/status
     /1410917919467491333?.

104 *"rather than lend legitimacy to poor policy"*: Editorial Board, "Opinion: Sha'Carri Richardson's relay exclusion wasn't necessary. USA Track and Field did it anyway," *Washington Post*, July 10, 2021, washingtonpost.com/opinions/2021/07/10/shacarri-richardsons-relay-exclusion-wasnt-necessary-usa-track-field-did-it-anyway.

104 *substances prohibited*: "Marijuana FAQ: Your Questions Answered," USADA, accessed October 8, 2021, usada.org/athletes/substances/marijuana-faq. See also "World Anti-Doping Code International Standard Prohibited List 2022," World Anti-Doping Agency, wada-ama.org/sites/default/files/resources/files/2022list_final_en.pdf.

104 *WADA believes*: Marilyn A. Huestis, Irene Mazzoni, and Oliver Rabin, "Cannabis in Sport: Anti-Doping Perspective," *Sports Medicine* 41, no. 11 (2011): 949–66, ncbi.nlm.nih.gov/pmc/articles/PMC3717337.

104 *The minimum penalty*: Draper and Macur, "Sha'Carri Richardson, a Track Sensation."

105 *not a performance enhancement*: Claire Maldarelli, "Is marijuana a performance-enhancing drug? The best evidence says no," *Popular Science*, July 2, 2021, popsci.com/science/marijuana-performance-enhancing-drug-evidence.

105 *"an overview of the research"*: Matt Richtel, "Science Doesn't Support Idea That Marijuana Aids Athletes' Performance," *New York Times*, last modified July 23, 2021, nytimes.com/2021/07/09/sports/olympics/marijuana-sports-performance-enhancing.html.

105 *Major League Baseball*: "MLB, MLBPA agree to changes to joint drug program," MLB, December 12, 2019, mlb.com/press-release/press-release-mlb-mlbpa-agree-to-changes-to-joint-drug-program.

105 *caffeine may enhance athletic endurance*: Matthew S. Ganio et al., "Effect of caffeine on sport-specific endurance performance: A systematic review," *Journal of Strength and Conditioning Research* 23, no. 1 (January 2009): 315–24, pubmed.ncbi.nlm.nih.gov/19077738.

107 *Is voting an ethics choice*: Susan Liautaud, *The Power of Ethics* (New York: Simon & Schuster, 2021).

109 *fewer than . . . 80,000 votes*: Philip Bump, "Donald Trump will be president thanks to 80,000 people in three states," *Washington Post*, December 1, 2016, washingtonpost.com/news/the-fix/wp/2016/12/01/donald-trump-will-be-president-thanks-to-80000-people-in-three-states.

109 *Al Gore lost*: "US election 2020: Does this compare to 2000 Florida recount?" BBC News, November 12, 2020, bbc.co.uk/news/election-us-2020-54903188.

109 *two elections in Georgia*: "Georgia Highlights: Democrats Win the Senate as Ossoff Defeats Perdue," *New York Times*, last modified May 11, 2021, nytimes.com/live/2021/01/06/us/georgia-election-re sults. See also "Georgia U.S. Senate runoff results," *Washington Post*, last modified January 19, 2021, washingtonpost.com/elections/elec tion-results/georgia-senate-runoffs-2021/.

CHAPTER 3: WORK

113 Financial Times *headline*: Madison Marriage, "Men Only: Inside the charity fundraiser where hostesses are put on show," *Financial Times*, January 23, 2018, ft.com/content/075d679e-0033-11e8-9650 -9c0ad2d7c5b5.

122 *Percentage of the group's work*: Max H. Bazerman and Dolly Chugh, "Decisions Without Blinders," *Harvard Business Review*, January 2006, hbr.org/2006/01/decisions-without-blinders.

124 *You are a bystander*: Susan Liautaud, *The Power of Ethics* (New York: Simon & Schuster, 2021).

127 *Restrictive voting*: Andrew Ross Sorkin and David Gelles, "Black Ex ecutives Call on Corporations to Fight Restrictive Voting Laws," *New York Times*, March 31, 2021, nytimes.com/2021/03/31/business/vot ing-rights-georgia-corporations.html.

127 *Black business leaders to sign a letter*: Associated Press, "CEOs gather to speak out against voting law changes," AP News, April 11, 2021, apnews.com/article/nfl-legislation-football-voting-rights-kenneth -frazier-0184a15a63fc2accfd5aeab973d341ae.

127 *spoke out over the new laws*: Matthew Impelli, "A Full List of Com panies That Have Advocated Against Georgia's New Voting Law," *Newsweek*, April 1, 2021, newsweek.com/full-list-companies-that -have-advocated-against-georgias-new-voting-law-1580435.

127 *Major League Baseball moved the Draft and the All-Star Game*: Va nessa Romo, "MLB Moves All-Star Game From Atlanta Over Geor gia's New Voting Law," NPR, April 2, 2021, npr.org/2021/04/02 /983970361/mlb-moves-all-star-game-from-atlanta-over-georgias -new-voting-law?t=1630252451349.

127 *"it wasn't our business"*: David Gelles, "'Our Menu Is Very Darwinian.' Leading McDonald's in 2021," *New York Times*, July 2, 2021, nytimes .com/2021/07/02/business/chris-kempczinski-mcdonalds-corner -office.html.

128 *Mitch McConnell*: Richard Cowan, "'Stay out of politics,' Republican

leader McConnell tells U.S. CEOs, warns of 'consequences,'" Reuters, April 5, 2021, reuters.com/article/us-usa-georgia-mcconnell-idUKKB N2BS1R8.

129 *"Where do we speak up on an issue?"*: Ibid.

137 *"Friendship is always a sweet responsibility"*: Kahlil Gibran, "Quotes," Goodreads, accessed December 1, 2021, goodreads.com/quotes /198892-friendship-is-always-a-sweet-responsibility-never-an-op portunity?page=4. See also personal.umich.edu/~jrcole/gibran/sand foam/sandfoam.html.

140 *the way the orchestra hired*: Anthony Tommasini, "To Make Orches- tras More Diverse, End Blind Auditions," *New York Times*, last mod- ified Aug 6, 2021, nytimes.com/2020/07/16/arts/music/blind-audi tions-orchestras-race.html.

140 *began using blind auditions*: Ibid.

140 *While this hiring system*: James Doeser, PhD, *Racial/Ethnic and Gender Diversity in the Orchestra Field*, League of American Orchestras, Sep- tember 2016, ppv.issuelab.org/resources/25840/25840.pdf, p. 3–4.

141 *New technology has facilitated*: Daniel Bortz, "Can Blind Hiring Im- prove Workplace Diversity?" Society for Human Resource Manage- ment, March 20, 2018, shrm.org/hr-today/news/hr-magazine/0418 /pages/can-blind-hiring-improve-workplace-diversity.aspx.

141 *AI in the experimental hiring tool*: Jeffrey Dastin, "Amazon scraps secret AI recruiting tool that showed bias against women," Reuters, October 10, 2018, reuters.com/article/us-amazon-com-jobs-automa tion-insight/amazon-scraps-secret-ai-recruiting-tool-that-showed -bias-against-women-idUSKCN1MK08G.

143 *Pew Research Center*: John Gramlich, "10 facts about Americans and Facebook," Pew Research Center, June 1, 2021, pewresearch.org/fact -tank/2021/06/01/facts-about-americans-and-facebook.

143 *LinkedIn . . . now has 800 million members*: "About LinkedIn," LinkedIn, accessed December 14, 2021, about.linkedin.com.

143 *99 percent*: Nora Ganim Barnes, PhD; Ashley Mazzola; and Mae Killeen, "Oversaturation & Disengagement: The 2019 Fortune 500 Social Media Dance," Center for Marketing Research, UMass Dart- mouth, last modified February 11, 2020, umassd.edu/cmr/research /2019-fortune-500.html.

143 *Many employers today use social media*: "Use of Social Media in Hiring," Justia, last modified October 2021, justia.com/employment /hiring-employment-contracts/use-of-social-media-in-hiring.

150 *"implicit bias" or "unconscious bias"*: Charlotte Ruhl, "Implicit or Un-

conscious Bias," Simply Psychology, July 1, 2020, simplypsychology
.org/implicit-bias.html.

151 *we're not as ethical in our decision making*: Max H. Bazerman and
Ann E. Tenbrunsel, *Blind Spots*: *Why We Fail to Do What's Right and
What to Do About It* (Princeton, NJ: Princeton University Press, 2011).

CHAPTER 4: TECHNOLOGY

155 *In a post dated January 7, 2021*: Mark Zuckerberg, "The shocking
events of the last 24 hours," Facebook, January 7, 2021, facebook
.com/zuck/posts/10112681480907401.

155 *In June 2021, Facebook announced*: "Facebook suspends Trump
until 2023, shifts rules for world leaders," Reuters, June 5, 2021,
reuters.com/world/us/facebook-suspends-former-us-president
-trumps-account-two-years-2021-06-04/.

155 *Jack Dorsey suspended Donald Trump's Twitter account*: Nitasha Tiku,
Tony Romm, and Craig Timberg, "Twitter Bans Trump's Account, Citing Risk of Furthering Violence," *Washington Post*, January 8, 2021,
washingtonpost.com/technology/2021/01/08/twitter-trump-dorsey.
See also "Permanent suspension of @realDonaldTrump," Twitter Inc.,
January 8, 2021, blog.twitter.com/en_us/topics/company/2020/sus
pension.

156 Packingham v. North Carolina: Packingham v. North Carolina, 582
U.S. (2017), supremecourt.gov/opinions/16pdf/15-1194_08l1.pdf.

156 *the Court recognized*: Stuart Benjamin, "Opinion: What is the 'do no
harm' position on the First Amendment in cyberspace?" *Washington Post*, June 19, 2017, washingtonpost.com/news/volokh-conspir
acy/wp/2017/06/19/what-is-the-do-no-harm-position-on-the-first
-amendment-in-cyberspace.

156 *First Amendment*: U.S. Const. amend. I, constitution.congress.gov
/constitution/amendment-1.

157 *calls for combat*: Maggie Haberman, "Trump Told Crowd 'You Will
Never Take Back Our Country with Weakness,'" *New York Times*,
last modified January 15, 2021, nytimes.com/2021/01/06/us/politics
/trump-speech-capitol.html.

159 *"It's my opinion"*: Taylor Swift, "For Taylor Swift, the Future of Music Is a Love Story," *Wall Street Journal*, last modified July 7, 2014,
wsj.com/articles/for-taylor-swift-the-future-of-music-is-a-love-story
-1404763219.

159 *released her album* 1989: Victor Luckerson, "This Is Why Taylor

Swift's Album Isn't on Spotify," *Time*, October 28, 2014, time.com
/3544039/taylor-swift-1989-spotify; Swift, "For Taylor Swift."

159 *new licensing deal*: Marc Schneider, "Spotify Signs Long-Term Deal
with Universal to Give Artists 'Flexible' Releases, Opens Door on
Windowing," *Billboard*, April 4, 2017, billboard.com/articles/business
/7751373/spotify-universal-music-new-albums-access-windowing
-licensing.

159 *Spotify compensates the rights holders*: "Streaming Numbers in
Context" and "How is streamshare calculated?" Loud & Clear, accessed October 5, 2021, loudandclear.byspotify.com.

160 *Artists are then compensated by the rights holders*: "How is streamshare calculated?" and "How is Spotify measuring payouts on this
site? Why doesn't this focus on what artists actually take home?"
Loud & Clear, accessed December 13, 2021, loudandclear.byspotify
.com/?question=how-is-stream-share-calculated.

160 *largest music-streaming service*: Omri Wallach, "Which streaming service has the most subscriptions?" World Economic Forum, March 10,
2021, weforum.org/agenda/2021/03/streaming-service-subscriptions
-lockdown-demand-netflix-amazon-prime-spotify-disney-plus-apple
-music-movie-tv.

160 *2021 third-quarter*: Spotify Investors, Financials, 2020 Q4 press
release, accessed December 31, 2021, s22.q4cdn.com/540910603
/files/doc_financials/2021/q3/Shareholder-Letter-Q3-2021_FINAL
.pdf.

160 *emerging artists may make very little*: Emily Blake, "Data Shows
90 Percent of Streams Go to the Top 1 Percent of Artists," *Rolling
Stone*, September 9, 2020, rollingstone.com/pro/news/top-1-percent
-streaming-1055005.

161 *streaming accounts for 84 percent*: Joshua P. Friedlander and Matthew Bass, "Mid-Year 2021 RIAA Revenue Statistics," Recording Industry Association of America, accessed December 13, 2021, riaa
.com/wp-content/uploads/2021/09/Mid-Year-2021-RIAA-Music
-Revenue-Report.pdf. See also Alan B. Krueger, "Streaming Is
Changing Everything," chap. 8 in *Rockonomics* (New York: Currency,
2019). See also Friedlander and Bass, "Year-End 2020 RIAA Revenue
Statistics," Recording Industry Association of America, accessed December 13, 2021, riaa.com/wp-content/uploads/2021/02/2020-Year
-End-Music-Industry-Revenue-Report.pdf.

161 *"boost to the music industry"*: Ibid.

161 *$75.5 million*: Friedlander and Bass, "Year-End 2020 RIAA Revenue."

164 *Facebook had ad revenue*: Facebook, Inc., "Facebook Reports Fourth Quarter and Full Year 2019 Results," PR Newswire, January 29, 2020, investor.fb.com/investor-news/press-release-details/2020/Facebook-Reports-Fourth-Quarter-and-Full-Year-2019-Results/default.aspx; Rishi Iyengar, "Here's how big Facebook's ad business really is," CNN Business, last modified July 1, 2020, cnn.com/2020/06/30/tech/facebook-ad-business-boycott/index.html.

164 *Facebook's share*: Megan Graham, "Digital ad spend grew 12% in 2020 despite hit from pandemic," CNBC, last modified April 7, 2021, cnbc.com/2021/04/07/digital-ad-spend-grew-12percent-in-2020-despite-hit-from-pandemic.html.

166 *Just under five feet tall*: Zorabots, accessed October 9, 2021, zorarobotics.be.

166 *she can interact with people*: Adam Satariano, Elian Peltier, and Dmitry Kostyukov, "Meet Zora, the Robot Caregiver," *New York Times*, November 23, 2018, nytimes.com/interactive/2018/11/23/technology/robot-nurse-zora.html.

166 *"accompany you throughout your day"*: "Zbos by Zora," Zorabots, accessed October 9, 2021, zorarobotics.be/zbos-zora.

166 *therapeutic companion robot*: "PARO Therapeutic Robot," PARO, accessed December 24, 2021, parorobots.com. See also Facebook, Inc., "Facebook Reports Fourth Quarter."

167 *South Korea stepped up its use of robots*: Arirang News, "S. Korean developers create AI robot to help prevent spread of COVID-19," video, June 13, 2020, youtube.com/watch?v=rTTI44cY4n8.

167 *more than 1.5 billion*: United Nations Department of Economic and Social Affairs, *World Population Ageing 2019: Highlights*, 2019, accessed September 11, 2021, un.org/en/development/desa/population/publications/pdf/ageing/WorldPopulationAgeing2019-Highlights.pdf.

168 *elderly share emotions more freely with robots*: Satariano, Peltier, and Kostyukov, "Meet Zora."

169 *David Hanson*: David Hanson, "On Humanoid Robots: Relationships, Rights, Risks and Responsibilities," interviewed by Susan Liautaud, Ethics Incubator, April 2019, ethicsincubator.net/ethics-and-truth-interviews/david-hanson-interview.

170 *Robert Julian-Borchak Williams*: Kashmir Hill, "Wrongfully Accused by an Algorithm," *New York Times*, last modified August 3, 2020, nytimes.com/2020/06/24/technology/facial-recognition-arrest.html.

170 *first known case*: Ibid.

171 *With good-quality photos*: Patrick Grother, Mei Ngan, and Kayee Hanaoka, "FRVT Part 2: Identification," National Institute of Standards and Technology, March 27, 2020, nvlpubs.nist.gov/nistpubs/ir/2019/NIST.IR.8271.pdf.

171 *the American Civil Liberties Union reported*: Jacob Snow, "Amazon's Face Recognition Falsely Matched 28 Members of Congress with Mugshots," ACLU, July 26, 2018, aclu.org/blog/privacy-technology/surveillance-technologies/Amazons-face-recognition-falsely-matched-28.

171 *embracing these FRT tools*: Shirin Ghaffary and Rani Molla, "Here's where the US government is using facial recognition technology to surveil Americans," *Vox*, last modified December 10, 2019, vox.com/recode/2019/7/18/20698307/facial-recognition-technology-us-government-fight-for-the-future.

171 *Amazon's FRT*: Snow, "Amazon's Face Recognition."

171 *study of gender and skin-color bias*: Joy Buolamwini and Timnit Gebru, "Gender Shades: Intersectional Accuracy Disparities in Commercial Gender Classification," *Proceedings of Machine Learning Research* 81: 1–15, 2018, proceedings.mlr.press/v81/buolamwini18a/buolamwini18a.pdf.

172 *ban police use of facial recognition technology*: Kashmir Hill, "How One State Managed to Actually Write Rules on Facial Recognition," *New York Times*, last modified March 5, 2021, nytimes.com/2021/02/27/technology/Massachusetts-facial-recognition-rules.html.

172 *Microsoft . . . won't sell facial recognition technology*: Jay Greene, "Microsoft won't sell police its facial-recognition technology, following similar moves by Amazon and IBM," *Washington Post*, June 11, 2020, washingtonpost.com/technology/2020/06/11/microsoft-facial-recognition.

172 *In 2020, Microsoft*: Washington Post Live (@PostLive), "Microsoft president @BradSmi says the company does not sell facial recognition software to police depts.," Twitter, June 11, 2020, twitter.com/postlive/status/1271116509625020417.

172 *Amazon . . . one-year moratorium*: Amazon Staff, "We are implementing a one-year moratorium on police use of Rekognition," Amazon, June 10, 2020, aboutamazon.com/news/policy-news-views/we-are-implementing-a-one-year-moratorium-on-police-use-of-rekognition. See also Drew Harwell, "Amazon extends ban on police use of its facial recognition technology indefinitely," *Washington Post*,

May 18, 2021, washingtonpost.com/technology/2021/05/18/amazon-facial-recognition-ban/.

172 *3 billion images*: Kate O'Flaherty, "Clearview AI's Database Has Amassed 3 Billion Photos. This Is How if You Want Yours Deleted, You Have to Opt Out," *Forbes*, January 26, 2020, forbes.com/sites/kateoflahertyuk/2020/01/26/clearview-ais-database-has-amassed-3-billion-photos-this-is-how-if-you-want-yours-deleted-you-have-to-opt-out/?sh=4ebd278360aa.

172 *More than six hundred law enforcement agencies*: Kashmir Hill, "The Secretive Company That Might End Privacy as We Know It," *New York Times*, last modified November 2, 2021, nytimes.com/2020/01/18/technology/clearview-privacy-facial-recognition.html.

172 *Facebook announced*: David Meyer, "After Facebook abandons facial recognition, the technology takes another blow with new Clearview AI ban," *Fortune*, November 3, 2021, fortune.com/2021/11/03/clearview-ai-Australia-facial-recognition-facebook/.

175 *State laws regarding posthumous privacy*: Natalie M. Banta, "Death and Privacy in the Digital Age," *North Carolina Law Review* 94, no. 3 (2016), scholarship.law.unc.edu/cgi/viewcontent.cgi?article=4765&context=nclr.

178 *"ready to listen"*: "Products & Pipeline," Woebot Health, accessed November 22, 2021, woebothealth.com/products-pipeline/. See also Arielle Pardes, "The Emotional Chatbots Are Here to Probe Our Feelings," *Wired*, January 31, 2018, wired.com/story/replika-open-source.

178 *works by inviting people*: "About us," Woebot Health, accessed November 22, 2021, woebothealth.com/about-us/.

178 *replacement for human connection*: "For users," Woebot Health, accessed November 22, 2021, woebothealth.com/for-users/.

178 *Replika*: "Our Story," Replika, replika.ai/about/story.

179 *downloaded more than 2 million times*: Pardes, "The Emotional Chatbots Are Here."

179 *FDA-approved cognitive therapy apps*: Christina Farr, "The FDA just approved the first app for treating substance abuse," CNBC, last modified September 14, 2017, cnbc.com/2017/09/14/the-fda-approved-the-first-mobile-app-to-treat-substance-use-disorders.html.

179 *more than 700,000 people die*: "Suicide," World Health Organization, June 17, 2021, accessed September 11, 2021, who.int/news-room/fact-sheets/detail/suicide.

179 *mental disorder*: "The World Health Report 2001: Mental Disorders

affect one in four people," World Health Organization, September 28, 2001, who.int/news/item/28-09-2001-the-world-health-report-2001 -mental-disorders-affect-one-in-four-people.

180 *Risks of bot therapy*: Amelia Fiske, Peter Henningsen, and Alena Buyx, "Your Robot Therapist Will See You Now: Ethical Implications of Embodied Artificial Intelligence in Psychiatry, Psychology, and Psychotherapy," *Journal of Medical Internet Research* 21, no. 5 (May 2019): e13216, ncbi.nlm.nih.gov/pmc/articles/PMC6532335.

182 *Alexa*: Susan Liautaud, *The Power of Ethics* (New York: Simon & Schuster, 2021).

182 *2.6 smart speaker devices*: "NPR and Edison Research Report: 60M U.S. Adults 18+ Own a Smart Speaker," NPR, January 8, 2020, npr .org/about-npr/794588984/npr-and-edison-research-report-60m-u -s-adults-18-own-a-smart-speaker.

183 *"hundreds of millions of Alexa-enabled devices"*: Ben Fox Rubin, "Amazon sees Alexa devices more than double in just one year," CNET, January 6, 2020, cnet.com/home/smart-home/amazon-sees -alexa-devices-more-than-double-in-just-one-year.

184 *Amazon notes in their terms of service*: "Alexa Terms of Use," Amazon, last modified September 28, 2021, accessed November 30, 2021, amazon.com/gp/help/customer/display.html?nodeId=201809740.

185 *On Monday, January 25*: Yun Li, "GameStop jumps amid retail frenzy, shares double at one point in wild trading," CNBC, January 25, 2021, cnbc.com/2021/01/25/gamestop-shares-jump-another-40per cent-shake-off-analyst-downgrade-as-epic-short-squeeze-contin ues.html.

185 *purchasing a lottery ticket*: Yun Li, "GameStop, Reddit and Robin-hood: A full recap of the historic retail trading mania on Wall Street," CNBC, last modified January 30, 2021, cnbc.com/2021/01/30/game stop-reddit-and-robinhood-a-full-recap-of-the-historic-retail-trading -mania-on-wall-street.html.

185 *stock price skyrocketed*: Yahoo Finance, GameStop Corp. (GME), NYSE - Nasdaq Real Time Price, Jan 2011–Jan 30, 2021, finance.ya hoo.com/quote/GME/history?.

185 *disconnected*: Li, "GameStop, Reddit and Robinhood."

185 *more than six times the previous single-day record*: Annabel Smith, "The Reddit revolt: GameStop and the impact of social media on institutional investors," The TRADE, April 13, 2021, thetradenews.com /the-reddit-revolt-gamestop-and-the-impact-of-social-media-on -institutional-investors.

186 *tenfold*: "What happened this week," Robinhood blog, January 29, 2021, blog.robinhood.com/news/2021/1/29/what-happened-this-week.

186 *Robinhood had to limit trading*: Li, "GameStop, Reddit and Robinhood."

187 *coffeehouse tour*: Ron Lieber, "Robinhood Hits Campus, Where Credit Card Companies Fear to Tread," *New York Times*, September 25, 2021, nytimes.com/2021/09/25/your-money/robinhood-colleges.html.

189 *Firing over one hundred rounds*: Rich Braziel et al., "Bringing Calm to Chaos: A critical incident review of the San Bernardino public safety response to the December 2, 2015, terrorist shooting incident at the Inland Regional Center," Critical Response Initiative, Washington, D.C., Office of Community Oriented Policing Services, 2016, justice.gov/usao-cdca/file/891996/download.

189 *Apple and the Justice Department had been sparring*: Adam Satariano and Chris Strohm, "The Behind-the-Scenes Fight Between Apple and the FBI," Bloomberg, March 20, 2016, bloomberg.com/news/features/2016-03-20/the-behind-the-scenes-fight-between-apple-and-the-fbi.

190 *Tim Cook issued a letter*: Tim Cook, "A Message to Our Customers," Apple, February 16, 2016, apple.com/customer-letter.

190 *FBI withdrew its request*: Ellen Nakashima and Reed Albergotti, "The FBI wanted to unlock the San Bernardino shooter's iPhone. It turned to a little-known Australian firm," *Washington Post*, April 14, 2021, washingtonpost.com/technology/2021/04/14/azimuth-san-bernardino-apple-iphone-fbi.

190 *Apple is now suing Azimuth*: Ibid.

190 *Apple claims*: "Answers to your questions about Apple and security," Apple website, accessed December 13, 2021, apple.com/customer-letter/answers.

191 *San Bernardino shootings*: Adam Nagourney, Ian Lovett, and Richard Pérez-Peña, "San Bernardino Shooting Kills at Least 14; Two Suspects Are Dead," *New York Times*, December 2, 2015, nytimes.com/2015/12/03/us/san-bernardino-shooting.html. See also Mark Berman, Elahe Izadi, and Wesley Lowery, "At least 14 people killed, 17 injured in mass shooting in San Bernardino, Calif.; two suspects killed in shootout with police," *Washington Post*, December 2, 2015, washingtonpost.com/news/post-nation/wp/2015/12/02/police-in-san-bernardino-calif-responding-report-of-shooting/.

191 *Apple came down on the side*: Kifi Leswing, "Apple's fight with

Trump and the Justice Department is about more than two iPhones," CNBC, last modified January 16, 2020, cnbc.com/2020/01/16/apple -fbi-backdoor-battle-is-about-more-than-two-iphones.html.

191 *"compromising the security"*: Cook, "A Message to Our Customers."

191 *"Apple deserves"*: Eric Lichtblau and Katie Benner, "Apple Fights Order to Unlock San Bernardino Gunman's iPhone," *New York Times*, February 17, 2016, nytimes.com/2016/02/18/technology/apple-timothy -cook-fbi-san-bernardino.html.

192 *"Apple cannot bypass your passcode"*: Orin Kerr, "Apple's dangerous game," *Washington Post*, September 19, 2014, washingtonpost.com /news/volokh-conspiracy/wp/2014/09/19/apples-dangerous-game; "Privacy," Apple, accessed September 13, 2021, apple.com/privacy /government-information-requests.

193 *first humanoid robot*: "Sophia the Robot," Her Future Summit, accessed September 21, 2021, herfuturesummit.org/speaker/sophia -the-robot; "Sophia," Hanson Robotics, accessed September 21, 2021, hansonrobotics.com/sophia.

193 *The Hanson Robotics website describes Sophia*: "Sophia," Hanson Robotics.

193 *Her face*: Susan Liautaud, *The Power of Ethics* (New York: Simon & Schuster, 2021). See also Jack Kelly, "Sophia—The Humanoid Robot—Will Be Rolled Out This Year Potentially Replacing Workers," *Forbes*, January 26, 2021, forbes.com/sites/jackkelly/2021/01/26 /sophia-the-humanoid-robot-will-be-rolled-out-this-year-potential ly-replacing-workers/?sh=4d9900806df2.

193 *"can estimate your feelings"*: "Sophia," Hanson Robotics.

193 *Sophia's artificial intelligence*: Ibid.

193 *Sophia continually learns*: Sara Brown, "Machine learning, explained," MIT Sloan School of Management, April 21, 2021, mitsloan.mit.edu /ideas-made-to-matter/machine-learning-explained.

193 *granted citizenship*: Zara Stone, "Everything You Need to Know About Sophia, the World's First Robot Citizen," *Forbes*, November 7, 2017, forbes.com/sites/zarastone/2017/11/07/everything-you -need-to-know-about-sophia-the-worlds-first-robot-citizen/?sh =186ebd4046fa.

193 *European Parliament*: Janosch Delcker, "Europe divided over robot 'personhood,'" *Politico*, April 11, 2018, politico.eu/article/europe -divided-over-robot-ai-artificial-intelligence-personhood; Mady Delvaux, *Report with recommendations to the Commission on Civil*

Law Rules on Robotics (2015/2103(INL)), European Parliament, January 27, 2017, europarl.europa.eu/doceo/document/A-8-2017-0005 _EN.pdf.

194 *letter to the EU*: "Open Letter to the European Commission: Artificial Intelligence and Robotics," open letter, robotics-openletter.eu.

CHAPTER 5: CONSUMER CHOICES

199 *Boohoo sold a bodycon minidress*: Sandra Laville, "The story of a £4 Boohoo dress: cheap clothes at a high cost," *The Guardian*, June 22, 2019, theguardian.com/business/2019/jun/22/cost-cheap-fast-fashion-workers-planet.

199 *vanilla spice latte at Starbucks*: "Starbucks UK Menu Prices," Fast Food Menu Prices, accessed September 11, 2021, fastfoodmenuprices .com/uk/starbucks-menu-prices-uk.

199 *"In 1991, the average American bought"*: United Nations Environment Programme, "Cleaning up couture: what's in your jeans?" December 14, 2018, unep.org/news-and-stories/story/cleaning-couture-whats -your-jeans.

199 *garments are later recycled*: Ibid.

199 *"landfill fashion"*: Jim Zarroli, "In Trendy World of Fast Fashion, Styles Aren't Made to Last," NPR, March 11, 2013, npr.org/2013/03/11 /174013774/in-trendy-world-of-fast-fashion-styles-aren't-made-to -last.

200 *"slow fashion"*: Audrey Stanton, "What Is Fast Fashion, Anyway?" Good Trade, accessed September 12, 2021, thegoodtrade.com/fea tures/what-is-fast-fashion.

200 *Fast fashion companies*: Shuk-Wah Chung, "Fast fashion is 'drowning' the world. We need a Fashion Revolution!" Greenpeace, April 21, 2016, greenpeace.org/international/story/7539/fast-fashion-is-drowning -the-world-we-need-a-fashion-revolution/. See also Terri Pous, "The Democratization of Fashion: A Brief History," *Time*, February 6, 2013, style.time.com/2013/02/06/the-democratization-of-fashion-a-brief -history.

200 *"3,781 liters of water"*: United Nations Environment Programme, "Cleaning up couture."

200 *"The fashion industry is responsible"*: United Nations Environment Programme, "UN Alliance for Sustainable Fashion addresses damage of 'fast fashion,'" March 14, 2019, unep.org/news-and-stories

/press-release/un-alliance-sustainable-fashion-addresses-damage
-fast-fashion. See also "How Much Do Our Wardrobes Cost to the
Environment?" World Bank, September 23, 2019, worldbank.org/en
/news/feature/2019/09/23/costo-moda-medio-ambiente.

206 *U.S. Department of Agriculture (USDA) says*: Miles McEvoy, "Organic
101: What the USDA Organic Label Means," United States Department of Agriculture, March 13, 2019, usda.gov/media/blog/2012/03
/22/organic-101-what-usda-organic-label-means.

207 *USDA categorizes organic products*: "About Organic Labeling,"
United States Department of Agriculture, ams.usda.gov/rules-regula
tions/organic/labeling.

207 *In 2020, organic food sales*: Dymond Green, "The rise of the organic
food market," CNBC, September 22, 2021, cnbc.com/2021/09/22
/organic-food-sales-surged-in-2020-higher-demand-and-cheaper
-costs.html; "U.S. Organic Industry Survey 2021," Organic Trade Association, accessed October 14, 2021, ota.com/market-analysis/or
ganic-industry-survey/organic-industry-survey.

207 *a 2012 in-depth study*: Crystal Smith-Spangler et al., "Are organic
foods safer or healthier than conventional alternatives?: a systematic review," *Annals of Internal Medicine* 157, no. 5 (September 2021):
348–66, pubmed.ncbi.nlm.nih.gov/22944875.

207 *Columbia University Climate School*: Anuradha Varanasi, "Is Organic
Food Really Better for the Environment?" State of the Planet, October 22, 2019, news.climate.columbia.edu/2019/10/22/organic-food
-better-environment.

208 *Peter Singer's point*: Jennie Richards, "Peter Singer: The Ethics of
What We Eat," Humane Decisions, August 1, 2016, humanedecisions
.com/peter-singer-the-ethics-of-what-we-eat.

208 *Twenty-five thousand people die of starvation*: John Holmes, "Losing
25,000 to Hunger Every Day," United Nations, un.org/en/chronicle
/article/losing-25000-hunger-every-day.

210 *working paper from Harvard Business School*: The final version of
their paper is at Benjamin Edelman and Michael Luca, "Racial Discrimination in the Sharing Economy: Evidence from a Field Experi-
ment," *American Economic Journal: Applied Economics*, April 2017,
9 (2): 1–22, www.aeaweb.org/articles?id=10.1257/app.20160213.

210 *Civil Rights Act of 1964*: *Know Your Rights: Title II of the Civil Rights
Act of 1964*, United States Department of Justice Civil Rights Divi-
sion, justice.gov/crt/page/file/1251321/download. See also Rebecca
Greenfield, "Study Finds Racist Discrimination by Airbnb Hosts,"

Bloomberg, December 10, 2015, bloomberg.com/news/articles/2015
-12-10/study-finds-racial-discrimination-by-airbnb-hosts.

211 *"There were lots"*: Brian Solomon, "Airbnb Confronts Racism As It
Hits 100 Million Guest Arrivals," *Forbes*, July 13, 2016, forbes.com
/sites/briansolomon/2016/07/13/airbnb-confronts-racism-as-it-hits
-100-million-guest-arrivals/?sh=64a036916b76.

214 *"Veganism"*: *Cambridge Dictionary*, s.v. "veganism," Cambridge University Press, accessed November 16, 2021, dictionary.cambridge.org
/us/dictionary/english/veganism.

214 *An "ethical vegan"*: Jordi Casamitjana, "The foundations of ethical
veganism," Vegan Society, December 18, 2020, accessed August 28,
2021, vegansociety.com/news/blog/foundations-ethical-veganism.

214 *According to the Vegan Society*: "Definition of veganism," The Vegan
Society website, accessed November 23, 2021, vegansociety.com/go
-vegan/definition-veganism.

215 *I focus here on the view*: Kelsey Piper, "A no-beef diet is great, but
only if you don't replace it with chicken," *Vox*, May 22, 2021, vox.com
/future-perfect/22430749/beef-chichen-climate-diet-vegetarian.

215 Stanford Encyclopedia of Philosophy: Tyler Doggett, "Moral Veg-
etarianism," *Stanford Encyclopedia of Philosophy*, September 14,
2018, plato.stanford.edu/entries/vegetarianism.

215 *"flexible vegan"*: "I am largely vegan but I'm a flexible vegan. I don't
go to the supermarket and buy non-vegan stuff for myself. But when
I'm travelling or going to other people's places I will be quite happy
to eat vegetarian rather than vegan." From Dave Gilson, "Chew the
Right Thing," *Mother Jones*, May 3, 2006, motherjones.com/politics
/2006/05/chew-right-thing/.

217 *rescinded the order*: "Rescission of Emergency Order of Prohibition," United States Department of Transportation Federal Aviation
Administration, November 18, 2020, faa.gov/foia/electronic_read
ing_room/boeing_reading_room/media/737_MAX_Rescission_of
_Grounding_Order.pdf.

217 *Boeing's 737 Max 8 and 9 planes*: "737 Max Updates, Current Products and Services," accessed October 14, 2021, boeing.com/commer
cial/737max.

217 *Disturbingly, Boeing knew*: Theo Leggett, "Boeing admits knowing of
737 Max problem," BBC News, May 6, 2019, bbc.co.uk/news/business
-48174797.

217 *Dennis Muilenburg personally called President Trump*: Keith Brad-
sher, Kenneth P. Vogel, and Zach Wichter, "Two-Thirds of the 737

Max 8 Jets in the World Have Been Pulled from the Skies," *New York Times*, March 12, 2019, nytimes.com/2019/03/12/business/boeing -737-grounding-faa.html.

217   *poor decisions by Boeing*: David Gelles and James Glanz, "Boeing Built Deadly Assumptions Into 737 Max, Blind to a Late Design Change," *New York Times*, June 1, 2019, https://www.nytimes.com /2019/06/01/business/boeing-737-max-crash.html.

218   *In rescinding the grounding of the planes*: Curtis Tate, "Boeing's troubled 737 Max cleared to fly again. When will travelers start boarding?" *USA Today*, November 18, 2020, eu.usatoday.com/story/travel /airline-news/2020/11/18/boeing-737-max-when-american-united -southwest-alaska-fly/3766105001; "Rescission of Emergency Order of Prohibition."

219   *"procedures were not completely followed"*: Peter Economy, "Boeing CEO Puts Partial Blame on Pilots of Crashed 737 MAX Aircraft for Not 'Completely' Following Procedures," *Inc.*, April 30, 2019, inc .com/peter-economy/boeing-ceo-puts-partial-blame-on-pilots-of -crashed-737-max-aircraft-for-not-completely-following-proce dures.html.

219   *fixing Boeing*: Natalie Kitroeff and David Gelles, "'It's More Than I Imagined': Boeing's New C.E.O. Confronts Its Challenges," *New York Times*, last modified March 6, 2020, nytimes.com/2020/03/05/busi ness/boeing-david-calhoun.html.

219   *"The objective is to get the Max up safely."*: Ibid.

225   *On April 23, 2013, deep cracks and fissures*: Nadra Nittle, "What the Rana Plaza Disaster Changed About Worker Safety," *Racked*, April 13, 2018, racked.com/2018/4/13/17230770/rana-plaza-collapse -anniversary-garment-workers-safety; Dana Thomas, "Why Won't We Learn from the Survivors of the Rana Plaza Disaster?" *New York Times*, April 24, 2018, nytimes.com/2018/04/24/style/survivors-of -rana-plaza-disaster.html.

225   *"Soldiers, paramilitary police officers"*: Julfikar Ali Manik and Jim Yardley, "Building Collapse in Bangladesh Leaves Scores Dead," *New York Times*, April 24, 2013, nytimes.com/2013/04/25/world/asia /bangladesh-building-collapse.html.

225   *Western fashion leaders*: Ibid.; Nittle, "What the Rana Plaza Disaster Changed"; and "5 years after the world's largest garment factory collapse, is safety in Bangladesh any better?" PBS News Hour, April 6, 2018, pbs.org/newshour/world/5-years-after-the-worlds-largest-gar ment-factory-collapse-is-safety-in-bangladesh-any-better.

225 *An investigation found*: Ibid.

226 *"The price pressure"*: Manik and Yardley, "Building Collapse in Bangladesh."

226 *"committed"*: Matthew Mosk, "Wal-Mart Fires Supplier After Bangladesh Revelation," ABC News, May 15, 2013, abcnews.go.com/Blotter/Wal-Mart-fires-supplier-bangladesh-revelation/story?id=19188673.

227 *work had been subcontracted out*: Manik and Yardley, "Building Collapse in Bangladesh."

229 *In 2002, the George W. Bush*: "Most Americans Now Can Prepare & File Taxes Online for Free Treasury, OMB, IRS launch new Free File Website," U.S. Department of the Treasury, January 16, 2003, home.treasury.gov/news/press-releases/kd3771.

229 *multiyear agreement*: "Free File: About the Free File Alliance," Internal Revenue Service, last modified April 8, 2021, irs.gov/e-file-providers/about-the-free-file-alliance.

229 *moderate-income filers*: Ann Carrns, "Navigating the Many Offers of Free Tax Help," *New York Times*, February 3, 2017, nytimes.com/2017/02/03/your-money/taxes/navigating-the-many-offers-of-free-tax-help.html.

229 *$72,000 or less*: "Free File: Do your Federal Taxes for Free," IRS, accessed November 19, 2021, irs.gov/filing/free-file-do-your-federal-taxes-for-free.

229 *60 million returns*: "About: The Free File Alliance: Serving the American Taxpayer," Free File Alliance, freefilealliance.org/about.

229 *Although 100 million Americans are eligible*: Carrns, "Navigating the Many Offers."

230 *paying customers*: Justin Elliott and Paul Kiel, "TurboTax and H&R Block Saw Free Tax Filing as a Threat—and Gutted It," ProPublica, May 2, 2019, propublica.org/article/intuit-turbotax-h-r-block-gutted-free-tax-filing-internal-memo.

230 *H&R Block dropped out*: Allyson Versprille, "IRS's Free File Partners Moving Forward Without H&R Block," Bloomberg Tax, June 18, 2020, news.bloombergtax.com/daily-tax-report/irss-free-file-partners-moving-forward-without-h-r-block.

230 *and in July 2021*: Carmen Reinicke, "Intuit will no longer be a part of an IRS program that helps millions of Americans file taxes for free," CNBC, last modified July 16, 2021, cnbc.com/2021/07/16/intuit-will-no-longer-participate-in-an-irs-free-tax-filing-program-.html.

230 *Britain and Japan don't require*: T. R. Reid, "Filing Taxes in Japan Is a Breeze. Why Not Here?" *New York Times*, April 14, 2017, nytimes

.com/2017/04/14/opinion/filing-taxes-in-japan-is-a-breeze-why-not -here.html. See also Binyamin Appelbaum, "Good Riddance, Turbo- Tax. Americans Need a Real 'Free File' Program," *New York Times*, July 19, 2021, nytimes.com/2021/07/19/opinion/intuit-turbotax-free -filing.html.

230 *In 2006, Austan Goolsbee*: Austan Goolsbee, "The Simple Return: Reducing America's Tax Burden Through Return-Free Filing," Brook- ings, July 1, 2006, brookings.edu/research/the-simple-return-reduc ing-Americas-tax-burden-through-return-free-filing/.

230 *chairman of President Obama's*: "Former Chairs of the Council of Economic Advisers," The White House: President Barack Obama, obamawhitehouse.archives.gov/administration/eop/cea/about/for mer-chairs.

230 *agreed not to compete*: Elliott and Kiel, "TurboTax and H&R Block."

231 *ProPublica revealed*: Ibid.

231 *Each company in the alliance*: Ibid. See also "Independent Assess- ment of the Free File Program," IRS, September 13, 2019, irs.gov/pub /newsroom/02-appendix-a-economics-of-irs-free-file.pdf.

233 *The word "philanthropy"*: Lexico, s.v. "philanthropia (*n.*)," accessed August 28, 2021, lexico.com/definition/philanthropia.

237 National Geographic *reports*: Laura Parker, "How the plastic bottle went from miracle container to hated garbage," *National Geographic*, August 23, 2019, nationalgeographic.com/environment/article/pla stic-bottles.

237 *2,000 times more expensive*: Matthew Boesler, "Bottled Water Costs 2000 Times as Much as Tap Water," *Business Insider*, July 13, 2013, busi nessinsider.com.au/bottled-water-costs-2000x-more-than-tap-2013-7.

238 *And the water will be healthier*: Brent A. Bauer, MD, "What is BPA, and what are the concerns about BPA?" Mayo Clinic, May 14, 2021, mayoclinic.org/healthy-lifestyle/nutrition-and-healthy-eating/ex pert-answers/bpa/faq-20058331.

CHAPTER 6: HEALTH

241 *waiting for organs*: "Organ Donation Statistics," Health Resources & Services Administration, last modified October 2021, organdonor .gov/statistics-stories/statistics.html.

241 *Organ donation, as described*: "Organ Donation and Transplanta- tion," Cleveland Clinic, last modified May 4, 2021, my.clevelandclinic .org/health/articles/11750-organ-donation-and-transplantation.

241 *There were 7,397 living donors*: "Organ donation again sets record in 2019," United Network for Organ Sharing, January 9, 2020, unos.org/news/organ-donation-sets-record-in-2019/.

241 *A single donor can supply organs*: "The Impact of One Organ Donor," University of Pittsburgh Medical Center HealthBeat, April 26, 2015, share.upmc.com/2015/04/the-impact-of-one-organ-donor.

241 *only 60 percent actually sign up*: "Organ Donation Statistics," Health Resources & Services Administration.

242 *Germany, like the U.S., uses an opt-in system*: Ghazi Ahmad and Sadia Iftikhar, "An Analysis of Organ Donation Policy in the United States," *Rhode Island Medical Journal* 99, no. 5 (May 2016): 25–27, rimed.org/rimedicaljournal/2016/05/2016-05-25-cont-ahmad.pdf.

242 *Austria . . . uses opt-out*: Richard H. Thaler, "Opting in vs. Opting Out," *New York Times*, September 26, 2009, nytimes.com/2009/09/27/business/economy/27view.html.

242 *Twenty countries in the European Union*: Nicole Scholz, *Organ donation and transplantation: Facts, figures and European Union action*, European Parliamentary Research Service, April 2020, europarl.europa.eu/RegData/etudes/BRIE/2020/649363/EPRS_BRI(2020)649363_EN.pdf.

243 *state of Illinois*: Thaler, "Opting in vs. Opting Out."

244 *sued NHS Trust*: The decision of Honourable Mrs. Justice Yip in ABC v (1) St. George's Healthcare NHS Trust, (2) South West London and St George's Mental Health NHS Trust, and (3) Sussex Partnership NHS Foundation Trust, 2020 EWHC 455 (QB), bailii.org/ew/cases/EWHC/QB/2020/455.html.

244 *Symptoms, according to the Mayo Clinic*: Mayo Clinic Staff, "Huntington's disease," Mayo Clinic, April 14, 2020, mayoclinic.org/diseases-conditions/huntingtons-disease/symptoms-causes/syc-20356117.

244 *With Huntington's disease*: "Huntington's Disease," National Organization for Rare Disorders, rarediseases.org/rare-diseases/huntingtons-disease.

244 *About 30,000 people in the U.S.*: Ibid.

244 *tested positive*: The decision of Honourable Mrs. Justice Yip.

247 *"freely and widely for scientific research"*: "The Importance of HeLa Cells," Johns Hopkins Medicine, accessed August 28, 2021, hopkinsmedicine.org/henriettalacks/importance-of-hela-cells.html.

247 *countless medical breakthroughs*: Ibid.

248 *who controls the cells taken*: "Henrietta Lacks: Science must right a

historical wrong," *Nature* 585, no. 7, nature.com/articles/d41586-020-02494-z.

248 *One hospital consent form*: "Consent to Operation, Procedure and Administration of Anaesthesia," Stanford Hospital and Clinics, stanfordhealthcare.org/content/dam/SHC/for-patients-component/womens-imaging/docs/15-01-consent-to-operation-admin-of-anesthesia.pdf.

248 *diverging views*: Rebecca Skloot, "Your Cells. Their Research. Your Permission?" *New York Times*, December 30, 2015, nytimes.com/2015/12/30/opinion/your-cells-their-research-your-permission.html.

248 *genetic information will be linked*: Ibid.

250 *Alzheimer's*: "Dementia," World Health Organization, accessed August 29, 2021, who.int/news-room/fact-sheets/detail/dementia. See also "What is Alzheimer's Disease?" Alzheimer's Association, accessed December 30, 2021, alz.org/alzheimers-dementia/what-is-alzheimers.

251 *Almost 6 million people*: "Minorities and Women Are at Greater Risk for Alzheimer's Disease," Centers for Disease Control and Prevention, accessed December 8, 2021, cdc.gov/aging/publications/features/Alz-Greater-Risk.html.

251 *more than 55 million people worldwide*: "Dementia," World Health Organization.

253 *"Imagine a world"*: Walter Isaacson, "Who Should Decide?" chap. 42 in *The Code Breaker: Jennifer Doudna, Gene Editing, and the Future of the Human Race* (New York: Simon & Schuster, 2021).

253 *"we might all go barreling down"*: Ibid.

254 *In contrast, so-called germline therapy*: "How Is Genome Editing Used?" National Human Genome Research Institute, last modified August 3, 2017, accessed October 3, 2021, genome.gov/about-genomics/policy-issues/genome-editing/how-genome-editing-is-used.

254 *"control of their own evolution"*: Jennifer A. Doudna and Samuel H Sternberg, "What Lies Ahead," chap. 8 in *A Crack in Creation: Gene Editing and the Unthinkable Power to Control Evolution* (Boston: Mariner Books, 2017).

255 *young sickle cell patient*: Walter Isaacson, "Thought Experiments," chap. 41 in *The Code Breaker: Jennifer Doudna, Gene Editing, and the Future of the Human Race* (New York: Simon & Schuster, 2021).

258 *NPR/Marist survey*: Geoff Brumfiel, "Vaccine Refusal May Put Herd Immunity at Risk, Researchers Warn," NPR, April 7, 2021, npr.org

/sections/health-shots/2021/04/07/984697573/vaccine-refusal
-may-put-herd-immunity-at-risk-researchers-warn.

258 *The CDC says*: Wesley H. Self, MD, et al., "Comparative Effective-
ness of Moderna, Pfizer–BioNTech and Janssen (Johnson & Johnson) Vaccines in Preventing COVID-19 Hospitalizations Among
Adults Without Immunocompromising Conditions—United States,
March–August 2021," *Morbidity and Mortality Weekly Report* 70,
no. 38 (September 24, 2021): 1337–43, cdc.gov/mmwr/volumes/70
/wr/mm7038e1.htm?s_cid=mm7038e1_w.

258 *All fifty states*: Drew DeSilver, "States have mandated vaccinations
since long before Covid-19," Pew Research Center, October 8, 2021,
pewresearch.org/fact-tank/2021/10/08/states-have-mandated-vac
cinations-since-long-before-Covid-19.

258 *officially eradicated*: "Region of the Americas is declared free of
measles," Pan American Health Organization, September, 27, 2016,
paho.org/hq/index.php?option=com_content&view=article&id=12
528:region-americas-declared-free-measles&Itemid=1926&lang=en.

261 *I learned that the imaging department*: "Medical Imaging," American
Hospital of Paris, accessed August 29, 2021, american-hospital.org
/en/our-specialties/imaging-center.

262 *According to the American Medical Association*: Michael J. Rigby,
"Ethical Dimensions of Using Artificial Intelligence in Health Care,"
AMA Journal of Ethics 21, no. 2 (February 2019): 121–24, journalof
ethics.ama-assn.org/article/ethical-dimensions-using-artificial-intel
ligence-health-care/2019-02.

262 *in addition to diagnosis*: Brian Kalis, Matt Collier, and Richard Fu,
"10 Promising AI Applications in Health Care," Harvard Business Review, May 10, 2018, hbr.org/2018/05/10-promising-ai-applications-in
-health-care.

262 *Accenture found that*: "AI: Healthcare's new nervous system," Accenture, accessed December 13, 2021, accenture.com/au-en/insights
/health/artificial-intelligence-healthcare.

263 *Medical ethics experts*: David Magnus, PhD, and Thomas A. Raffin,
email message to author, October 19, 2020.

263 *diabetic retinopathy*: Cade Metz, "India Fights Diabetic Blindness
with Help from A.I.," *New York Times*, March 10, 2019, nytimes.com
/2019/03/10/technology/artificial-intelligence-eye-hospital-india
.html. See also Christina Farr, "Google launches India program
to screen diabetics for eye conditions that can cause blindness,"

CNBC, last modified February 25, 2019, cnbc.com/2019/02/25/google-verily-launch-diabetic-eye-condition-screening-tech-in-india.html.

263 *eleven eye doctors in India for every 1 million people*: Ibid.

264 *facial recognition technology*: Robert Glatter, MD, "AI Can Read a Cardiac MRI in 4 Seconds: Do We Still Need Human Input?" *Forbes*, September 28, 2019, forbes.com/sites/robertglatter/2019/09/28/ai-can-read-a-cardiac-mri-in-4-seconds-do-we-still-need-human-input/#220ca676a401.

265 *"Every flavor Skittle compressed into one"*: Sabrina Tavernise, "Use of E-Cigarettes Rises Sharply Among Teenagers, Report Says," *New York Times*, April 16, 2015, nytimes.com/2015/04/17/health/use-of-e-cigarettes-rises-sharply-among-teenagers-report-says.html.

265 *The most popular e-cigarette in the U.S.*: Jamie Ducharme, "Tobacco Giant Altria Just Made a $12.8 Billion Investment in Juul," *Time*, December 20, 2018, time.com/5485247/juul-altria-investment.

265 *In 2016, it became illegal*: Ned Sharpless, MD, "How FDA Is Regulating E-Cigarettes," U.S. Food and Drug Administration, last modified September 10, 2019, fda.gov/news-events/fda-voices/how-fda-regulating-e-cigarettes.

265 *legal age to twenty-one*: "Newly Signed Legislation Raises Federal Minimum Age of Sale of Tobacco Production to 21," U.S. Food and Drug Administration, January 15, 2020, fda.gov/tobacco-products/ctp-newsroom/newly-signed-legislation-raises-federal-minimum-age-sale-tobacco-products-21.

265 *CEO of Juul Labs*: "Juul CEO Tells Non-Smokers Not to Vape or Use His Company's Product," CBS News, last modified August 29, 2019, cbsnews.com/news/juul-ceo-kevin-burns-tells-non-smokers-not-to-vape-or-use-his-companys-product.

265 *on October 12, 2021*: "FDA Permits Marketing of E-Cigarette Products, Marking First Authorization of Its Kind by the Agency," U.S. Food & Drug Administration, October 12, 2021, fda.gov/news-events/press-announcements/fda-permits-marketing-e-cigarette-products-marking-first-authorization-its-kind-agency.

266 *"if credible evidence emerges"*: Ibid.

266 *Dr. Norman E. Sharpless*: Sharpless, "How FDA Is Regulating E-Cigarettes."

266 *harmful to children*: "Is It Safe to Vape Around Children?" Johns Hopkins All Children's Hospital, accessed August 29, 2021, hopkins

allchildrens.org/Patients-Families/Health-Library/HealthDocNew/Is
-It-Safe-to-Vape-Around-Children.

267 *advertising and promotion*: "Tobacco Industry Marketing," Centers for Disease Control and Prevention, last modified May 14, 2021, accessed November 26, 2021, cdc.gov/system/files/documents/reports/federal-trade-commission-cigarette-report-2019-smokeless-tobacco-report-2019/2019_smokeless_tobacco_report.pdf.

267 *doing both interchangeably*: Blaha, "5 Vaping Facts."

269 *21,000 donor organs*: "The Kidney Project," University of California San Francisco, accessed August 29, 2021, pharm.ucsf.edu/kidney/need/statistics.

270 *higher success rate*: "What is living kidney donation?" NHS Blood and Transplant, accessed August 29, 2021, organdonation.nhs.uk/become-a-living-donor/donating-your-kidney/what-is-living-kidney-donation.

276 *"The privilege of a lifetime"*: *A Joseph Campbell Companion: Reflections on the Art of Living*, ed. Diane K. Osbon (New York: Harper Perennial, 1995).